IN HELL BEFORE DAYLIGHT

The Siege and Storming of the Fortress of Badajoz, 16 March to 6 April 1812.

Based on the eye-witness accounts of the men of the French and British armies.

The Duke of Wellington.

IN HELL
BEFORE DAYLIGHT

*The Siege and Storming of the Fortress
of Badajoz, 16 March to 6 April 1812*

Ian Fletcher

*'The capture of Badajoz affords as strong an instance
of the gallantry of our troops as has ever been displayed.
But I greatly hope that I shall never again be the
instrument of putting them to such a test . . .'*
Wellington

*'In short, I think the capture of Badajoz a very
extraordinary event; and I should be much at a loss to
account for it in any manner consistent with
probability.'*
General Léry, Army of the South

SPELLMOUNT
Staplehurst

British Library Cataloguing in Publication Data:
A catalogue record for this book is available
from the British Library

Copyright © Ian Fletcher 1984, 1994

ISBN 1-873376-26-X

First published in the UK in 1984 by
Spellmount Limited
The Old Rectory
Staplehurst
Kent TN12 0AZ

New Edition 1994

3 5 7 9 8 6 4 2

Printed in Great Britain by
St Edmundsbury Press Limited, Bury St Edmunds, Suffolk.

Contents

Foreword   vii

1   The Peninsula to 1812   1

2   Preparations   7

3   Investment   25

4   The Storm   54

5   Aftermath   97

6   Epilogue   116

Badajoz Today   118

Appendix   I   The Anglo-Portuguese Forces   120

Appendix   II   The French Garrison   122

Appendix III   British Casualties   124

Appendix IV   Thanks from Parliament   127

Glossary of Siege Terms   129

Bibliography   131

Index   133

Foreword

This book is a documentation of the siege of Badajoz in Spain, which took place during the Peninsular War. Together with Ciudad Rodrigo it was one of the great fortress cities which commanded the two routes between Portugal and Spain. They were the 'Keys of Spain'. Rodrigo was the first to fall, in January 1812, and the following month Wellington's men began to slip away southwards to lay siege to Badajoz. The city had been attacked twice before by the British but a lack of proper siege materials had caused both attempts to be abandoned. This time, however, they hoped to be 'third time lucky'.

The conditions in which the British soldiers worked, fought and died, as they worked their way in trenches towards the walls of Badajoz, were not unlike the miseries suffered and endured by another British army, in Flanders, just over a hundred years later. The rain poured incessantly for days whilst the men worked without proper tools as the enemy guns took their toll.

The story of the siege and of the storming and sacking that followed reads, in places, like a horror story as the victorious British troops, driven to a point of madness by the fury of their onslaughts and the violence of the fighting, found vent, as Oman wrote, 'in misconduct far surpassing that which would have followed a pitched battle where the losses had been equally as great'.

Many accounts were left for us by the participants and it is upon these that this book is based. On the French side the main account is that written by Colonel Lamare, chief engineer in Badajoz, who left us a detailed account of the conditions inside the town during the siege. On the British side a host of officers and men left us their accounts of the siege, some detailed and some not so detailed. For the operations in general the major sources were the works of Oman, Napier and Fortescue, and Gerwood's Dispatches. The real story, however, lies in the pages of memoirs of the eye-witnesses, of the men who were there, the men who took part in and experienced one of the most glorious, bloody and most shameful deeds in the history of the British army. James MacCarthy printed his *Storming of Badajoz* in 1836, and is entirely concerned with the siege, whilst others such as Kincaid, Grattan, Costello and Simmons, to name a few, devoted lengthy passages of their memoirs to it. These are the accounts that matter, those of the ordinary soldier.

For the technical side of the operations most of the information can be found in Jones' *Sieges in Spain and Portugal, 1808–1814*, which contains details of working parties, supplies and day-by-day progress reports from the trenches, and the *Dickson Manuscripts*, which give details of the operations carried on by the artillery.

This book is solely concerned with the siege from the beginning on 16 March to the storming on the 6 April and the sacking afterwards. Therefore only a brief outline is given of the operations of the British forces under Hill and Graham, which were acting as covering forces to the besiegers and were to prevent any interference by the French armies, particularly those of Marmont and Soult, who wasted so much time between them that they, through their indecision, probably cost Badajoz any chance it might have had of being relieved. Also, only a brief outline is given of the events in the Peninsular both before and after the siege.

All the information used in writing this book can be found in the works listed in the bibliography at the back. Therefore, I have sought not to litter the pages with notes or any other references in order to concentrate on writing a straightforward account of one of the more horrific chapters in the history of the British army.

Ian Fletcher.

1

The Peninsula to 1812

When Napoleon first sent Junot to occupy Portugal and then set up his brother as King of Spain, savage revolts broke out in both countries. The rising was remarkably successful at first in Spain where a French force surrendered at Baylen and as a result of this the British government decided to act to help the two countries. They had at their disposal a force of trained troops, mainly in Ireland, under Sir Arthur Wellesley, the victor of Assaye and Argaum. Although disliked by other officers of the army who considered him a 'Sepoy General', he was given command. Wellington, as we shall now call him, although he gained that title later on, was a master of strategy and tactics. His instrument was the army, largely remodelled and trained in individual combat and musketry at Hythe and Shorncliffe by Sir John Moore.

Wellington landed on the Portuguese coast north of Lisbon which stands on the peninsula, with the Atlantic to the west and the wide estuary of the Tagus to the south-east. If Wellington could trap Junot on the Lisbon peninsular he could soon starve him out. This forced Junot to attack but the new British tactics of steady musketry against mass French charges which were used here, at Vimiero, gave Wellington the victory. That should have been the end for Junot and his army, but an elderly General named Burrard landed in Portugal and superseded Wellington, and the next day an even older General, Dalrymple, took over command from Burrard. Dalrymple decided that any further action was unneccesary and so he agreed to the Convention of Cintra, whereby it was agreed that Junot and his army would be given free passage back to France unmolested. Following this, all three British generals were recalled to England to explain before a court of enquiry how they had allowed the French army to escape back to France.

Meanwhile, the British army in Portugal was put under the command of Sir John Moore. His plan of campaign was based on assurances given by the Spanish that all Spain was ready to rise against Napoleon, who had come in person to enforce his brother's authority, provided substantial British help was to be had. Moore undertook the risk of striking inland from the coast, right across Napoleon's lines of communication, with Madrid as his eventual objective. If the Spanish had risen the plan might have been successful. Moore, however, did not know the Spaniards. They

The Battle of Corunna, 1809. Sir John Moore is carried away dying as the British Army retreat to the ships waiting in the harbour. After this battle Wellington was given command of the Army in the Peninsula.

were very brave, proud and touchy and very dilatory, never doing today what they could leave until tomorrow. Moreover, there was no effective insurgent Spanish government. The 'Juntas' or committees which sprang up everywhere claiming to act in the name of the absent King were composed of jealous local magnates; each appointed his own general and each general regarded it as beneath his dignity to obey any other general, while all Spanish generals regarded it as beneath their dignity to accept orders from an English heretic. They would discuss Moore's suggestions and then carry out what they had already determined upon without any consideration of Moore's plans.

As a result of this there were a number of badly managed revolts while Napoleon secured Madrid. Moore, waiting at Salamanca, now had to decide either to retreat, which would leave a hopeless situation, or to advance which might force Napoleon to move against him, and thus allow the Spaniards to reorganise their revolts against the French. He chose the second course. Napoleon duly moved against the British but the promised Spanish risings either did not occur or went off badly and were easily suppressed.

2

ROYAL ARTILLERY.

Gunners of the Royal
Artillery, 1812.

Consequently, Moore, in the depth of winter, was forced into a fighting retreat towards Corunna. This was the most suitable Spanish port where transports could be assembled to withdraw the British army. The retreat was carried out, but so closely pursued was Moore's army that he had to turn and fight at the point of embarkation, and at the battle fought at Corunna in January 1809, Moore himself was killed. The bulk of his army, however, was safely evacuated to the waiting ships.

Meanwhile, the court of enquiry had cleared Wellington who returned to Portugal to command the British forces there. The year 1809 saw a series of swift actions planned to drive the French out of Portugal, in order to secure the British base. The first to be dealt with was Marshal Soult, who had secured northern Portugal. The Battle of the Douro was a masterly Wellington operation. He secured some boats by a piece of expert reconnaissance when the French were sure he could do nothing of the sort. With these boats he ferried his men across the Douro, caught Soult by surprise and drove him out of Portugal.

Wellington's next move was south against a strong French force

3

under Jourdain and Victor which was moving down the Tagus. Linking up with the Spanish under General Cuesta he attacked the French at Talavera. The result was a British victory inasmuch as the line of retreat to Portugal was secured. The battle also taught Wellington two lessons. The first was that although the Spanish troops were good guerilla fighters they were unreliable in a pitched battle. Cuesta's troops did very little at Talavera and it was said that they retreated at the noise of their own muskets. The second lesson learned was that it was useless to rely on Spanish promises of transport and supplies. The retreating British army nearly starved for want of these, despite profuse Spanish promises, perhaps sincere enough at the time they were given, but it was nobody's business to see that actual arrangements were made to fulfil the promises. By the end of 1809 the British position in the Peninsula had become serious. The defeat of Austria had left France free to concentrate on driving the British army into the sea. Wellington himself had other ideas, however, and had devised a plan intended to starve the French whilst his own army sat back secure behind strong defensive lines. This position was known as the lines of the Torres Vedras, a strong fortified position in some places thirty feet high, which was built across the Lisbon peninsula, and built so secretly that Massena, the French commander, had no idea of what was going on before him. To the north of these works the Portuguese people were forced or persuaded to clear the countryside, destroying crops and driving in livestock. Napoleon's armies always lived off the land in which they were campaigning, in contrast to the British soldiers, for Wellington had become an expert at keeping his men well supplied and fed with the least possible inconvenience to the local population. This meant that the French would find it hard to find food and supplies.

Wellington's plan worked as he had expected it to. Massena had little difficulty seizing the frontier fortresses of Portugal, and thrust Wellington's armies back towards Lisbon. At one point, where a mountain ridge blocked the only available road, Wellington made a stand and fought the battle of Busaco. Wellington's infantry was deployed in a line stretched across a wide front and their controlled and accurate musketry broke up the French attacks, driving their columns back over the ridge. The French had to advance in deep columns up narrow valleys, and as the head of each column debouched on the ridge it was exposed to the full fury of the best musketry in the world, and simply broke up before it had time to change.

Wellington, however, had no intention of standing. Busaco was intended to cause as much damage to the French as possible, and to delay further their pursuit. After the battle. Wellington retired to his prepared lines which Massena only discovered when he came face to face with them, and there he held out against repeated French

4

The Peninsular War
1808-1814

The Peninsula

attacks. Meanwhile, since no supplies were to be had from the surrounding countryside, and few could be carried laboriously from distant France, the French army starved, while the British army continued to be well supplied from the port of Lisbon.

Had the French marshals in Spain combined to deal with the British they could have made their position in Portugal impossible. Two things prevented this, however, and Wellington was aware of both. If any French commander evacuated his area of the peninsula in order to concentrate against the British there would be an immediate revolt of the local population, and a rebuke from Napoleon as a result. The other factor was that most of the French marshals were jealous of each other. Therefore Soult, in southern Spain, who could have made Wellington's position in Lisbon impossible, would not take any effective steps to aid Massena, whom he detested. He did, however, take the key fortress of Badajoz, but then retired to Seville, where there had been signs of a possible revolt, and did nothing further.

Wellington chose this moment to move and Massena was forced to move northwards. A mixed force of British and Portuguese troops

5

under Beresford was sent to attack Badajoz, which they did with little success and nearby was fought the fierce battle of Albuera.

Wellington himself was involved in two major battles on the Portuguese border, Sabagul and Fuentes d'Onoro, with the result that Massena had to retire from Portugal. Wellington then joined forces with Beresford and again assaulted Badajoz and was again unsuccessful. He had neither proper siege guns nor trained sappers and when Marmont brought his forces to join those of Soult, Wellington had to abandon the siege.

As the year 1812 began, large numbers of French troops were withdrawn from Spain for Russia and supplies diverted. Wellington was now offered a chance to take the offensive and this he did. His plan was first to secure the main roads in and out of Portugal and then thrust directly at Madrid, Joseph's capital. He felt that if this plan succeeded the Spaniards might, at last, make a properly concerted rising. Even if this did not happen, Wellington could retire to his base in Portugal and try again when another chance offered.

The two powerful fortresses which guarded the Spanish-Portuguese border had first to be dealt with and this Wellington proceeded to do in two of the fiercest struggles of the Peninsular War. Early in 1812 he captured Ciudad Rodrigo in the north, and by a swift move concerted with Beresford in command of an Anglo-Portuguese army, Wellington struck southward and laid siege once more to Badajoz. This is the story of that siege.

2

Preparations

Rodrigo had fallen and once again Wellington turned his attention to the fortress city of Badajoz. The preparations for the siege began in January with Alexander Dickson travelling to Setubal to take a large part of the siege train southwards by sea and road. Wellington's plan involved tricking the French into believing that he still had a large force on the frontier at Leon where his infantry and cavalry were, whereas his guns were on their way southwards. Wellington himself remained at his headquarters at Freineda until 5 March in order to deceive Marmont further into believing that the Allied army was still concentrated there. From 19 February onwards, however, Wellington's divisions began to slip away, one by one, to march on Badajoz and when he himself left, only the 5th Division and Victor Alten's cavalry brigade remained. The rest of the army were on their way to Elvas by way of Sabugal, Castello Branco, Villa Vehla and Niza. By 8 March the long column of infantry was cantoned in different places behind Elvas, with the 1st Division joining them on 10 March. The only troops not yet to arrive were the 5th Division who were expected by 16 March and two Portuguese brigades which were due to arrive around 20 March. With these two exceptions the whole of Wellington's field army was concentrated near Elvas by 16 March. In order that the French did not detect the disappearance of his army, which they would surely do if only Portuguese and Spanish cavalry were to be seen, Wellington kept the 1st Hussars of the King's German Legion, under Victor Alten, in the outposts in front of Ciudad Rodrigo.

After making arrangements with regard to affairs in that area, Wellington left his headquarters at Freineda on 5 March and, travelling by way of Castello Branco and Portalegre, he reached his new headquarters at Elvas on 12 March. He was now quite satisfied with his situation, with the larger part of his army having already arrived and the remainder arriving fast. As well as this, much of the siege material had arrived intact having survived the rough journey by sea and along the rocky mountain roads. The material which had been moved by road consisted of sixteen 24-pounder howitzers, which had started their journey on 30 January, and a convoy of 24- and 18-pounder travelling carriages and stores which had set off on 2 February. The former had arrived at Elvas on 25 February and the latter on 3 March. This was quite an achievement inasmuch as the

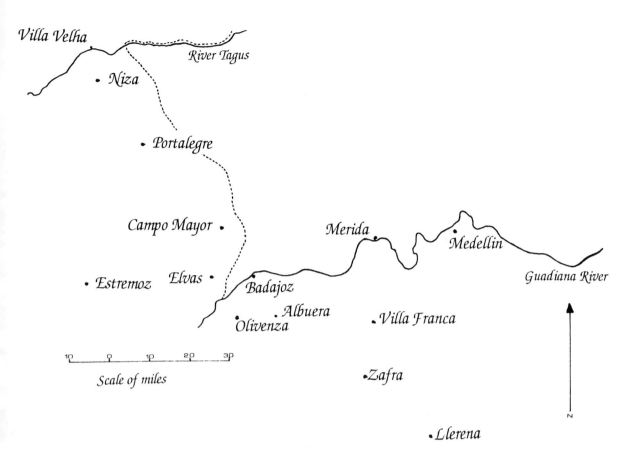

Operations around Badajoz

journey was over mountainous roads in the most rainy season of the year. The guns which had travelled by sea had also enjoyed a trouble-free passage away from winter storms. Alexander Dickson, on his arrival at Setubal on 10 February, found that the 24-pounders from Oporto had arrived thirty-six hours ahead of him and on 14 February he had begun to start to transport them by river boat to Alcacer do Sol from whence they would be hauled by oxen to Elvas along with their ammunition. The only problem Dickson encountered concerned the complementary train of twenty 18-pounder ship guns which Wellington had asked Admiral Berkley, commanding the squadron in Lisbon, to lend him. These guns turned out to be Russian and Dickson complained that they were not the same calibre as the British 18-pounders and would not take its shot. The only vessel in Lisbon harbour with British-made 18-pounders was the Admiral's flagship but he refused to hand these over. Dickson was forced to make do with the Russian guns for which, fortunately, a store of suitable ammunition was eventually found, although many had to be rejected as being unsuitable.

On 8 March all fifty-two guns of the siege train were reported

8

Elvas, Portugal. It was here that the British Army assembled before marching on Badajoz.

ready, and the officer commanding the Portuguese artillery in Elvas declared that he had found six old heavy English iron guns from the time of George II which had been stored there since General Burgoyne's expedition back in 1761.

While the siege guns had been gathered together, the garrison at Elvas had been busy for weeks making fascines and gabions which were now ready, as was a large consignment of cutting tools from the Lisbon arsenal and a train of twenty-two pontoons. The material was now ready and complete. The list of tools and stores for the siege of Badajoz included the following:

Shovels	1,000
Spare helves	150
Pick-axes	1,200
Spare helves	300
Spades	300
Tarpaulins, large	20
Tarpaulins, small	20
Spikes, 7 inch	6,000
Spikes, 10 inch	1,000

Saws, hand	30
Saws, pit	12
Saws, crosscut	6
Setters and files for the above, a good proportion	
Adzes, carpenters	30
Claw hammers, large	30
Claw hammers, small	30
Gimblets, spike	40
Gimblets, common	20
Spun yarn, coils	12
Hambro line, skeins	20
Hand hatchets	300
Hand bills	500
Sledge hammers	20
Tallow, firkins	2
Grease, kegs	6
Chalk, a small quantity	
Chest of tools, carpenters	2
Sand-bags, bushel	80,000
Broad-axes	60
Felling axes	300
Miners tools for twenty miners	
Levels with lines and bobs	6
Smiths tools for ten smiths	
Forge carts, complete	2
Steel, cwts	2
Coals, cauldrons	1
Nails, of sizes	20,000
Planes, of sorts	6
Gouges	20
Augers, of sizes	20
Compasses, pairs	20
Chalk lines, with reels	10
Box rulers, 2 feet	20
Oil stones	6
Wood squares	10
Wood levels	10
Iron squares	5
Ballast baskets	100
Hand-crow levers, 6 feet	10
Hand-crow levers, 5½ feet	10
Tents, complete for officers	10
Tents, complete for men	10
Fascine chokers	12
Fascine mallets	40

Badajoz on the Guadiana, as approached from Alberquerque and Elvas.

Scaling ladders, joints	36
Dark lanthorns	12
White rope coils, 2½ inch	2

In addition to these stores, a further 300 hand hatchets, 500 hand bills, 12 fascine chokers, 30 hand saws, 12 coils of spun yarn and 300 felling axes were to be ferried across to Aldea Gallega to be transported on carts to Elvas.

These then were the tools. The methods by which Wellington hoped to take Badajoz had changed little since the days of Vauban, the great French engineer of the 18th century. A besieging army would consist of a force large enough to carry on the actual siege whilst at the same time provide a covering force of sufficient strength to oppose any relieving army which might interfere. Having gathered this force the besiegers would establish supply and storage dumps as well as engineer and artillery parks, and would then set about digging a large trench parallel to that part of the fortifications which was to be breached. This trench or parallel would be dug at about maximum cannon range and would be strengthened with gabions and woolpacks. Having established this first parallel, along which men and supplies could be moved freely, sheltered from any fire from the town, a zig-zag or communication trench would be pushed forward and batteries constructed. About halfway towards the objective a second parallel would be dug and more batteries constructed. Sometimes a third and even a fourth parallel was dug. A sizable guard was needed in the trenches to repel any sortie by the besieged garrison.

11

Contemporary plan of
Badajoz from Jones' *Journal*
of the sieges . . .

Opposite:

A–B Cross-sections through breaches
C–D Cross-sections through breaches
E–F Cross-sections through breaches
G San Pedro bastion
H San Trinidad bastion
I Santa Maria bastion
J Unfinished ravelin
K Lunette Picurina
L Lunette San Roque
M Gate La Trinidad
N Four guns loaded with grape to
   sweep the breach
O Shells Placeo before breaches
P Boat in which was placed a company
   to enfilade the breach
Q British trenches
R Breaching batteries
S Inundation
T Houses destroyed during the siege
   to clear ramparts

The trenches would be pushed on until they reached a point at which the guns would be effective, a point at which it would also be safe for the besiegers to work. When this point had been reached they would begin a heavy bombardment of the bastions until breached.

The breaching batteries themselves consisted of fifty-two heavy guns, sixteen of which were 24-pounders, a further twelve were 24-pounder howitzers, and the remainder were the twenty Russian 18-pounders. The main task of breaching the walls fell to the 24-pounders, enormous guns with barrels nine feet long. For these guns alone 22,367 round shot were available as well as 24,983 rounds of other calibres. During the course of the siege Wellington's artillery were to use 2,253 barrels of gunpowder and with each barrel weighing ninety pounds that figure represents a lot of firing.

Each of the 24-pounder guns was capable of firing a fairly large iron ball twenty times an hour and after each firing it had to be dragged about eight feet back to its position after recoiling. Firing was of use only during the hours of daylight and, unless there was a breeze, it took thirty seconds for the black smoke to clear before it could be fired again.

Accuracy was vital, although the method of aiming the guns was nothing more than a case of pointing the barrel at the target and adjusting it accordingly. Each shot was aimed at a selected spot with

12

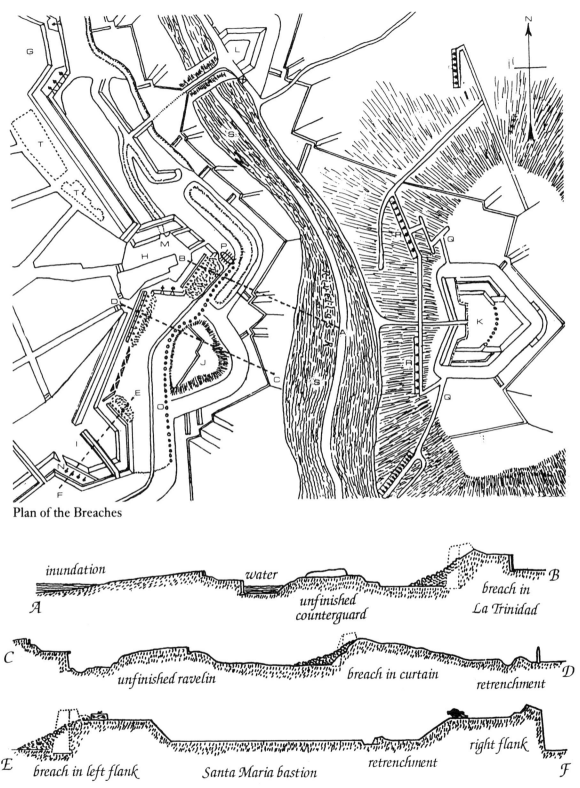

Plan of the Breaches

inundation

water

*breach in
La Trinidad*

A

B

*unfinished
counterguard*

C

unfinished ravelin

breach in curtain

retrenchment

D

E

breach in left flank

Santa Maria bastion

retrenchment

right flank

F

Cross section through Breaches

13

the intention of bringing down the wall forward into the ditch at the foot of it. This would mean that not only would there be a gap in the wall but the rubble would, theoretically, fill up the ditch and enable the storming soldiers to approach the breach a little easier up a gentle slope.

It was customary for the garrison to surrender with honour when the breaches became practicable. However, during the Peninsular War, garrisons had begun to fight on rather than capitulate. If a storming was necessary the defenders could expect no mercy from the besiegers, especially if many casualties had been sustained.

Wellington had at his disposal a force of about 300 British and 500 Portuguese artillerymen which he placed under the command of Alexander Dickson, and as well as these men there were fifteen British officers, five German Legion and seven Portuguese officers, again to come under Dickson's command. The Portuguese gunners were drawn from the 3rd or Elvas Regiment, while the British were drawn from the companies of Holcumbe, Gardiner, Glubb and Rettberg. The senior engineer was Colonel Richard Fletcher who had with him 115 men of the Royal Military Artificers, present at the start of the siege, and a party which came up from Cadiz during the final days. This was a vast improvement on the state of things in 1811 but the numbers were still far too small for an operation of this size. There were still no trained miners, and the volunteers from the line acting as sappers were for the large part unskilful, receiving just a basic training from the artificers. Only 120 men of the 3rd Division who had been at work at Ciudad Rodrigo were anything like efficient. The engineer arm was the weakest point in the siege and soon after the fall of Rodrigo, Wellington wrote to Lord Liverpool suggesting that a permanent unit, trained in the method of siege warfare, should be created as soon as possible.

'I would beg to suggest to your Lordship,' he wrote, 'the expediency of adding to the Engineer establishment a corps of sappers and miners. It is inconceivable with what disadvantage we undertake a siege, for want of assistance of this description. There is no French corps d'armée which has not a battalion of sappers and a company of miners. We are obliged to depend for assistance of this sort upon the regiments of the line; and, although the men are brave and willing, they want the knowledge and training which are necessary. Many casualties occur, and much valuable time is lost at the most critical period of the siege.'

Despite this the situation on 12 March seemed favourable. It was only fourteen miles from Elvas, where the siege train lay and the materials stored and ready, to Badajoz. Wellington had sufficient troops with him not only to invest the place but also to form a covering army, should Soult attempt to move against him. Wellington also believed that his advance would surprise the

14

A view of Badajoz from the North bank of the Guadiana.

French. Only Drouet's two divisions were in Estremadura and it would take them some weeks to gather enough reinforcements to be able to act with any effect. If Soult decided to march, then he would have to take men away from Grenada and the Cadiz lines, and unless he could raise the siege of Cadiz or evacuate Grenada he would not be able to gather more than 25,000 men and it would take him a few weeks to do that. Even if Soult were to gather his forces and march on Badajoz he could be fought with little risk. Unlike 1811, when he had only three Anglo–Portuguese infantry divisions and three British cavalry regiments, Wellington now had with him eight infantry divisions, nine when the 5th Division arrived at Elvas, and fourteen cavalry regiments. This meant that Wellington could fight Soult in a pitched battle with 40,000 men whilst still leaving 15,000 troops to invest Badajoz.

The only dangerous possibility was that Marmont might decide to intervene with five or six divisions from the army of Portugal as he had done before in June 1811, during the operations on the Caya. Although Wellington thought this probable, he knew he could count on at least three or four weeks of freedom from interruption from Marmont. What Wellington did not know, however, was that Napoleon had forbidden Marmont to move and it was only on 27 March that the marshal was granted permission to move, by which time it was too late.

15

Castle

St. Pedro   St. Antonio

Rivillas

Lunette

St. Roque

N.º 3   e   N.º 6   n   N.º 12
f

Fort Christor

GUADIANA

Attack
OF
BADAJOS,
BY
n. the Earl of Wellington,
th between the
17 March & 6.th April
1812.

Scale of Feet

See Sections.
Fig. 5.6.& 7. Plate X.

The possibility of Marmont's interference, however, made the operation against Badajoz a time problem for Wellington. If possible the place must be taken sometime in the first week in April, the earliest date at which any attempt at relief could be made. By 14 March every preparation had been completed and the pontoon train with its escort rolled out of Elvas and halted on the Guadiana, four leagues from Badajoz. Two days later, on 16 March, the 3rd, 4th and Light Divisions crossed the river. The march on Badajoz had begun.

Badajoz, capital of Estremadura, is situated on the left bank of the Guadiana river and stands in the midst of a fertile country. Before the war its population had been 16,000, but was now greatly reduced owing to the previous sieges by both the French and British armies. Most of the richer families had left in order to avoid the dangers of the war and famine, and with the appearance of Wellington's army families of all the different classes packed up their belongings and left the city. Old men, women and children could be seen loaded up with their property, some with waggons or carts, streaming away along every road, as Lamare wrote: 'they quitted their homes in tears, and often looked back with regret on their unhappy city, which they saw was about to be exposed a third time to all the calamities inseparable from war.' By the time the siege began only about four or five thousand people remained in the city. The governor of Badajoz was General Armand Phillipon. He enlisted in the Bourbon army in 1778 and by 1790 had risen to the rank of sergeant-major. During the following years he saw service in Italy, Switzerland and Hanover, and had served with the Grand Armée from 1805–07 and fought at Austerlitz. He was transferred to Spain in 1808 and fought at Talavera and at the siege of Cadiz. He was made a baron in 1810 and promoted to general de brigade. He was made governor of Badajoz in March 1811, and repulsed both Beresford's and Wellington's earlier siege attempts and was promoted to general de division in July of that year.

The fortifications of Badajoz formed an enclosure of nine bastions, each named after a saint but for the time being called by a number. These nine bastions were joined together by walls, with bastion no. 1 connected to the castle by way of the river front on the town's northern side, with the castle itself serving as a citadel with bastion no. 9 joining it on it's other side. The whole of this enclosure had a good revetment, the height of which varied from 19½–46 feet and was surrounded by a covered way with a counterscarp revetted to a height of 5–6½ feet except in front of the curtain between bastions 8 and 9, and in front of the latter, where there was neither ditch nor counterscarp but only a simple covered way.

On the right bank stood three outworks: the fort San Christobal, the Tête du Pont and the lunette Verlé, the latter being constructed

Illustrated on previous pages
The Attack on Badajoz. A contemporary plan showing the British lines and the main points of attack. From Jones' *Journal of the Sieges*

18

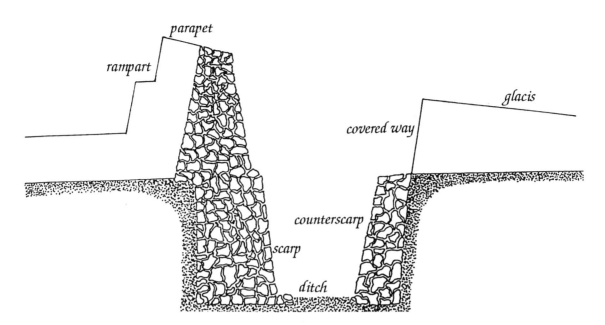

Some points of a typical fortification

only a short time previous to the siege. These works were linked to the city by means of an old stone Roman bridge and, in cases of emergency, by ferry-boat which had been established between the city and the San Christobal. On the left bank was built the fort Pardeleras, in front of bastions nos. 4 and 5, and in front of bastion no. 7 was built the strong lunette Picurina. The lunette San Roque covered the communication of the gate of la Trinidad.

When the British laid siege to Badajoz in 1811 they directed their efforts against the San Christobal and the castle, and because of this Soult had ordered this side of the fortress to be strengthened. He directed the lunette Verlé to be built upon the same spot where the British batteries had been positioned when they were used against the San Christobal. The ditches of this lunette were excavated to a depth of 14½ feet and were cut perpendicularly in the rock by means of blasting. A powder magazine and a timber bomb-proof for fifty men were constructed in a traverse and the gorge was closed by a strong loop-holed wall. The artillery armed it with the necessary armaments and projectiles and it was finished in September 1811. It commanded the surrounding ground well and was named Verlé in commemoration of the general of that name who fell at Albuera.

The breaches made by the British in the San Christobal had been repaired, the ditches deepened by blasting the rock, the counterscarps were made higher with masonry and the glacis raised to cover the scarps. Supplies of materials had been formed inside to be used to construct a powder magazine, a cistern and an arched bomb-proof barrack. The Tête du Pont, which had also suffered a great deal during the last siege had also been repaired. The work at these vital points went on without interruption and with so much

19

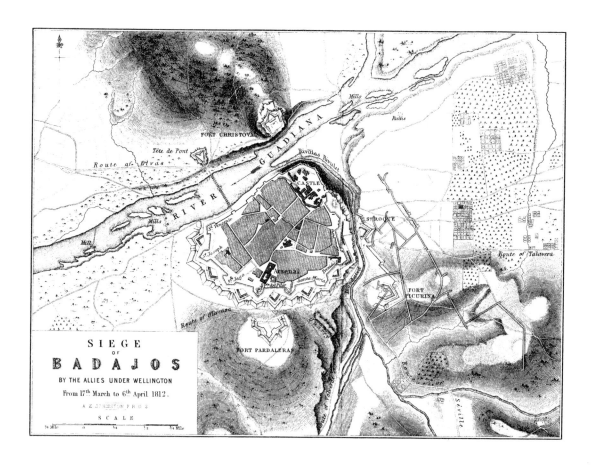

SIEGE
OF
BADAJOS
BY THE ALLIES UNDER WELLINGTON
From 17th March to 6th April 1812.
A.K.JOHNSTON F.R.G.S
SCALE

activity that by the time the British army appeared much of the work had been completed to the garrison's satisfaction.

On the left bank the crown work of Pardaleras, which had been nothing but a mass of rubbish when the French army took possession of Badajoz, had been raised from its ruins and vastly improved. The gorge was closed by a good loop-holed wall, the ditches deepened, the demi-bastion and the curtain on the right had been raised in order to see in reverse the approaches against fronts nos. 1, 2 and 3 between the fort and the Guadiana. The powder magazine and a bomb-proof barrack for the commandant and his garrison were rebuilt on their former foundations. The covered way was repaired and newly palisaded and the fort generally given the strength and solidity that time would allow, to withstand assault. The breach made by the French back in 1811, in the curtain between bastions 3 and 4, was also repaired and the trenches used by them in that first siege were levelled.

20

British Riflemen. 60th and 95th Regiments.

The ravelin between bastions 2 and 3 had been thrown up towards the end of 1811. Its revetments were now finished and the earth formed to it's proper shape. The artillery had armed this ravelin in such a way that this side of the fortress was considered greatly strengthened. The ravelins of bastions 1, 2, 3 and 4 were begun in February 1812, when the first reports of a possible siege began to arrive. The French troops of the garrison were the only workmen who could be depended upon and they worked hard and fast to raise the revetment of the ravelin between bastions 1 and 2 to over five feet above the foundations, this mass of earth having already a height of three feet over the glacis. The ravelin between bastions 3 and 4 were constructed entirely of earth, for the want of better materials, and likewise began to have some command over the glacis. These works were carried out under the command of Captain Lefaivre, of the engineers, who showed great skill and endeavour throughout the operations.

A cunette of 6½ feet deep and as many wide was started in the

21

Badajoz. A view of the west side of the town. From a watercolour by Captain C. G. Elliscombe.

ditch of the body of the fortress from bastion 1 to no. 3. In spite of the works, however, bastions 1, 2 and 3 were still considered by the French to be the weakest point in the defences and they had every reason to suspect this point would bear the main brunt of Wellington's assault. Therefore, as a final move the French formed galleries and branches at each salient of the counterscarp in order to be able, if necessary, to place mines beneath the batteries and in the terreplains of the bastions for the purpose of destroying the works if the British should take them. This plan was later dropped, however, due to the acute shortage of powder later in the siege.

Before the fronts nos. 7, 8 and 9 the French constructed two batardeaux in masonry with sluices, one in the ditch of the left face of the San Roque, and the other beneath the bridge over the Rivellas at the gorge of the San Roque. Together these formed the false lake or inundation which would cramp the British in their assaults and cause them great problems.

While the work on the fortifications progressed, the French artillery were busy arming the batteries and opening up new embrasures as well as constructing traverses to guard against enfilade. Together with the engineers they had established a workshop in which were prepared the various weapons and devices to be used in the defence of the place during the siege and the assault.

22

The central part of the defence, the castle, had been carefully prepared. Magazines and provisions were stored inside and the garrison's main powder magazine established there. The breach made by Beresford during the first siege had been completely repaired. The existing batteries were overhauled and put in good order and new ones constructed. The miners had been busy working on the rock upon which the castle stood to increase the height of its scarp. Its walls, which were 19½–46 feet high, were built on a rock and towered more than 60 feet above the waters of the Rivellas which flowed below them. This citadel was considered by all to be the strongest and most secure part of the defence and was to be the last place of refuge for the garrison if the British should penetrate the walls of the town.

Inside the town itself the barracks had been repaired and extended, as was the military hospital. Blinds had still to be made, as the town was completely devoid of the material needed to make them, and the nearest forest was too far away and transport virtually non-existent. The French troops had problems in other areas too. The job of digging and carrying the stones from the nearby quarries for their lime was difficult and prevented them from having sufficient stone for their needs. They had to dig up the roots of olive trees, which had been burnt in the previous sieges, to make charcoal. The shortages of timber meant that it was impossible to restore all of the palisades in the covered ways which had been destroyed in 1811. The timber for this purpose was to be found in a forest which was too distant and this shortage meant that the castle could not be fully palisaded, which would be favourable to the British.

In 1811 the besieging British troops had burned all the houses and all the corn in the neighbourhood. The peasants had fled and the land remained uncultivated. Therefore, Phillipon ordered the land to be ploughed and sown to within a circle of 300 yards of the town. The kitchen gardens which had been abandoned were assigned to different corps, and were to be cultivated to the best of their ability. All steps were taken to ensure that the garrison would be in a state sufficient to supply itself during the siege. A few days before the investment began, Chief of Battalion Truilhier, of the Engineers, arrived with Captain Meynhart, Lieutenant Vallon, fifty sappers, a detachment of the 64th Regiment, and twenty-five men of the 21st Regiment of the Chasseurs à Cheval, commanded by Lieutenant Raulef. As well as these troops, a convoy of about sixty mules loaded with flour also arrived.

The garrison itself consisted of 4,000 troops with about a further 400 men laid up in hospital. This number was considered too few to ensure a good strong defence, given the extent of the town and the outworks which had to be defended. Bastions 1 and 2 would be held by the 9th Light Infantry. Bastions 3 and 4 by the 28th Light Infantry, the 58th Regiment would hold bastion no. 5 and the 103rd Regiment were placed in bastions nos. 6 and 7. The castle and bastions 8 and 9 were entrused to the German troops, the Hesse d'Armstadt Regiment. The detachment of Spanish troops in the service of King Joseph were posted at the gate of Las Palmas, as were the men of the armed civil departments. The 88th Regiment and the small number of cavalry were placed in reserve in the Place de San Juan. The detachment of the 64th Regiment was attached to the artillery and the fifty sappers were to be used as gunners. The governor also formed a special company of men from the best marksmen in each battalion and were to harass the British troops working in the trenches. This company was organised by General Veiland and was commanded by Lieutenant Michel of the 9th Light Infantry and Leclerc de Ruffey of the 58th Regiment. Governor Phillipon then decided which officers would command the outworks. Colonel Pineau would command Pardaleras, Colonel Gaspard Thierry was placed in command of the lunette Picurina and Captain Villain would be in charge of the San Christobal. The castle in Badajoz would be under the command of Colonel Knoller.

Thus we have the state of Badajoz and the French garrison at the time of Wellington's approach.

3

Investment

At about nine o'clock on the morning of 16 March the warder at the top of the tower in the castle gave the signal that the British army had appeared on the Elvas road. The engineers threw a pontoon bridge across the Guadiana about four miles from the town and soon 12,000 men of the 3rd, 4th and Light Divisions, under Beresford, had crossed the river and were advancing along the left bank of the Guadiana towards the town. General Veiland immediately advanced to reconnoitre them with a small force before retiring to within the safety of the town walls at about two o'clock. The British column crossed the Olivenza road, passed behind the Sierra del Viento, extended to the Albuera road and halted to take up its position to begin the investment. They met with no opposition, and in fact Colonel Fletcher, commanding the Engineers, was able to inspect the town from the slopes of the Cerro de San Miguel, a short distance away. Soon afterwards all communication between the garrison in Badajoz and the main French army ceased. The siege had begun.

On the evening of 17 March, 3,000 troops broke ground about a thousand yards from the lunette Picurina. The night was wet, dark and stormy and the sound of the picks and shovels was drowned by the tempestuous roar of the high winds.

'The elements on this occasion adopted the cause of the besieged,' wrote Kincaid:

'for we had scarcely taken up our ground when a heavy rain commenced and continued without intermission for about a fortnight . . . and the duties in the trenches were otherwise rendered extremely harassing.'

Nevertheless, the soldiers, accustomed to such fatigues, set about opening a parallel near the height of San Miguel about 600 yards long and about 300 yards from the lunette Picurina and when the French peered through the mist next morning they saw with surprise that the British had completed the first parallel of their works. Phillipon had placed outposts in front of La Picurina but the officer in command of this drew back his men as the British approached without making any stand and without even making a report of it to the Governor. Through this Wellington had gained at least one night's work without loss.

An aerial shot, taken from a balloon in 1914. (1) is the Santiago bastion, (2) is the San Jose (3) is the San Vincente bastion, escaladed by Leith's 5th Division, and (4) is the wall breached by the French in an earlier siege.

In spite of a heavy fire directed upon the trenches by field pieces in the town and from La Picurina the parallel was extended 450 yards towards the Talavera road on 18 March.

The rain continued to fall heavily throughout the day filling the trenches with water resulting in extreme discomfort for the troops working in them. Kincaid again:

'We had a smaller force employed than at Rodrigo and the scale of operations was so much greater that it required every man to be in the trenches six hours every day and the same length of time every night which with the time required to and from them, through fields more than ankle deep in a stiff mud, left us never more than eight hours out of the twenty-four in camp and we never were dry the whole time.'

Siege work was loathed by the soldiers who regarded entrenching as 'navvy's work'. The discomfort in hiding from the French artillery and musket fire in cramped positions was looked upon as skulking, even though it was necessary. And not only were the rank and file forced to do a task which they hated but they were expected to do it without the aid of proper engineer's tools. The spade was rendered useless by the cold rain which turned the soil into a liquid mud which ran away in streams as it was shovelled up onto the parapets. It refused to pile up and consequently gave little or no cover at all and the slime offered little resistance to the musket fire from the garrison.

The atmosphere in the trenches soon became depressive and the British troops, in trying to add a touch of bravado to the proceedings, often exposed themselves more than was necessary. After spending his first morning in the camp James McGrigor wanted to see what the men were doing in the trenches and after breakfasting with Captain Thompson of the 88th, he went to visit the trenches:

'We were very soon obliged to creep on all fours as we advanced, for there were sharpshooters on the lookout who popped at every head that appeared and who, as it seems, were good marksmen, for they had killed many of our men in this way. Under the care of my friend Thompson, we returned in safety; but what was my horror when less than two hours after this, an officer of the 88th came to me with the information that our poor friend Thompson had been shot through the head while engaged with a friend in the same manner as he had but so lately been with me. An officer of another regiment had called upon him immediately after his return from the trenches with me, and had also expressed a wish to see the state of the trenches; Thompson offered to accompany him, and they proceeded but a short way, when Thompson, in bravado, stood up, looking directly at the spot from whence the shot came every now and then, believing he was out of reach, when he was struck on the head by a bullet, and fell dead.'

27

Badajoz. A view from the Picurina. From a watercolour by Captain C. G. Elliscombe.

The sporting instinct of the British officer still found vent, however; indeed Harry Smith managed to find time to go hare coursing with his dog, whilst a Captain in the Engineers challenged the French to prove their marksmanship whilst marking out ground for no. 7 battery. The battery was situated near a wall which was always lined with French soldiers waiting for someone to shoot at.

'He used to challenge them to prove the perfection of their marksmanship,' wrote James MacCarthy, 'by lifting up the skirts of his coat in defiance, several times in the course of his survey; and then deliberately measuring the ground by prescribed paces, driving stakes, setting spades etc; and when he had finished his task, make his conge, by again lifting the skirts of his coats and taking off his hat, amidst their ineffectual firing at him, although a soldier of our working party close to the captain was struck in the act of stooping, by a ball on the pouch belt where it crosses the bayonet belt behind. The man screamed with agony and the French laughed; but on examining him, he was found only to have been hurt by the concussion, both belts and the coat having been cut through as if with a penknife, without touching his skin.'

Apart from the appalling weather and the uncomfortable conditions endured by the British troops the tasks assigned to them often proved to be equally unpleasant. One particularly hazardous duty was that which was assigned to the best marksmen in each battalion.

28

These picked men were sent out independently into fox-holes, dug at night between their own batteries and the walls of the town. From these rifle pits these marksmen were to pick off any French soldiers who might expose themselves along the walls or at any of the gun-embrasures. Quite often, however, it would be these marksmen who would fall victim to the French sharpshooters. This in turn would prove to be dangerous for the men sent out to relieve them, for whilst looking for these holes, they might find them occupied by a dead or wounded comrade, and whilst trying to remove the body, without cover, the relief exposed himself to the French and ran a great risk of being shot at himself.

Another unpleasant task was performed by parties of men assigned to go out and recover dismembered limbs which had been scattered about by bursting shells. Costello thought that this was necessary 'in order to prevent any ill-effect their appearance might have on the courage of the Portuguese, whose prognostications were as likely to put their heels in motion as their heads'.

Kincaid likened trench-work to nothing better than serving an apprenticeship as a grave-digger or a game-keeper, as he said he found ample time for spade and rifle. The duties in the trenches were conducted by Major-Generals Colville, Bowes and Kempt, under the superintendence of General Picton, each remaining on duty for twelve hours and exposing themselves to great danger.

29

British troops begin digging the first parallel on the eastern side of Badajoz.

Indeed, Picton narrowly avoided death when a shell fell upon a man in a trench nearby, which exploded and 'scattered the man in fragments to the wind'.

Sergeant William Lawrence left this description of the conditions in the trenches before Badajoz:

'About eight hundred of us were every night busily engaged in the trenches, whilst a large number, who were called the covering party, were on the look-out in case of an attack by the enemy. The rain poured down so fast that balers were obliged to be employed in places, and at times the trenches were in such a state of mud that it was over our shoes. We were chiefly employed during the day in finishing off what we had done in the night, as very little else could be done then owing to the enemy's fire. We had not been to work many days before we got within musket shot of a fine fort situated a little distance from the town, and garrisoned with four or five hundred of the enemy, who annoyed us rather during our operations. One night as I was working in the trenches near this place, and just as the guards were about to be relieved, a shell from the town fell amongst them and exploded, killing and wounding about thirty. I never saw a worst sight of its kind, for some had their arms and legs, and some even their heads, which was worse, completely severed from their bodies.'

On 19 March they cut across the Talavera road and extended their parallel to within 200 yards of the lunette San Roque. To check this rapid advance Governor Phillipon ordered a sortie to be made against the works. At midday two battalions of 500 men each and about forty cavalry marched out unseen through the Trinidad gate under the command of General Veiland. They marched in column, wheeled into line and moved quickly against the works. Grattan was in the trenches that day:

'and having a little more experience than the officer who commanded the party, I observed with distrust the bustle which was apparent, not only in the fort of Picurina, but also along the ramparts of the town. Without waiting the formality of telling the commanding officer what I thought, I, on the instant, ordered the men to throw by their spades and shovels, put on their appointments, and load their firelocks. This did not occupy more than three minutes, and in a few seconds afterwards the entire trenches to our right were filled with Frenchmen, the workmen massacred, and the works materially damaged; while at the same moment, several hundred men attempted to throw themselves into the battery we occupied.'

With the sudden appearance of the French troops the workmen fled and the French began to demolish the parallel. The cavalry, commanded by Lieutenant Lavigne of the 26th Dragoons, turned the parallel at a gallop and pursued the fugitives as far as their bivouacs.

Lieutenant John Cooke was working in the trenches and having an argument with a friend who suddenly:

'shouted with an oath that the French were coming on, and instantly sprang out of the trench like a tiger, following his comrade, just such another fine fellow. Two or three French dragoons at that instant fired their pistols into the trenches, having approached within a few yards without being perceived. We had just entered the mouth of the parallel, and all joined in a simultaneous attack on the enemy's infantry, without regard to trenches or anything else. The French being beaten out of the advanced lines, retired and formed line under the castle, having two field pieces on their right flank. I cannot say how they entered the town, there was so much smoke covering them when near the walls. Phillipon knew his business well.'

In the course of the attack William Lawrence had expended all his ammunition, when suddenly a French sergeant came over the top of the trench and made a thrust at him with his bayonet:

'and while in the act of thrusting he overbalanced himself and fell. I very soon pinioned him to the ground with my bayonet, and the poor fellow soon expired. I was sorry afterwards that I had not tried to take him prisoner instead of killing him, but at the time we were all busily engaged in the thickest of the fight, and there was not much time to think about things.

31

And besides that, he was a powerful-looking man, being tall and stout, with a beard and moustache completely covering his face, as fine a soldier as I have seen in the French army, and if I had allowed him to gain his feet, I might have suffered for it; so perhaps in such times my plan was best – kill or be killed.'

As he lay on the floor of his tent, Private William Brown of the 45th heard an unusual firing at the works, and the cry of 'a sortie, a sortie' went up:

'Immediately standing to our feet, every man seized his pouch and musket, and without orders, rushed to the works. The enemy consisted of two thousand men, part of whom actually entered the trenches. Amongst the rest I perceived one fellow, a grenadier, with a handful of iron rods and a hammer, with which, no doubt, it was intended to spike our cannon, but they were soon driven into the town with considerable loss, when a heavy cannonade was commenced from the ramparts. On leaving the trenches, a man of our company had a narrow escape from a cannon ball which passed over his head, so near that it took away the crown of his cap as neatly as it had been done with a knife, and so dexterously that his cap was not removed from his head.'

The sortie was repulsed with a loss to the French of twenty men killed and 147 wounded, as well as thirteen officers wounded. The British casualties were around 200, most of whom were cut down in the trenches. Amongst these casualties was Colonel Fletcher, chief engineer, who was seriously wounded when a musket ball struck him in the groin, forcing a dollar-piece from his purse an inch into his thigh. He was confined to his tent for fourteen days, his duties being taken over by Majors Squire and Burgoyne, though Wellington gave orders that he remain in charge and Fletcher was consulted daily. Another of the casualties was Captain Cuthbert of the Fusiliers, one of Picton's aides. Cuthbert was rallying some of the workmen when a shot from the Picurina struck him on the hip which killed his horse and mangled the lower part of his body 'in a most frightful and fatal manner'.

Another important blow to the British was the loss of about 200 badly needed entrenching tools. Phillipon knew how important these were and had offered to pay high bounties for them.

With the sortie repulsed, order was restored and the work in the trenches was continued under a hail of musket and artillery fire. The French artillery in the town was directed with great accuracy and skill. Phillipon had placed a guard of several soldiers in the square tower of the church in the town, and by climbing onto the cross-beams they could see the besieging troops working in the trenches. During the changeover of work parties the relief troops and those who were to return to camp would both be in the trenches at the

Hussars and Infantry of the Duke of Brunswick's Oels Corps, 1812. A small number of these infantry fought for Wellington at Badajoz.

same time. On seeing this the French guards in the tower warned their artillery by ringing the bells and a tremendous fire of shot and shell would be poured into the trenches, often causing heavy casualties amongst the two or three thousand British troops crowded together in the works. Consequently, the relief was ordered not to enter until all the other men had left.

James MacCarthy and his comrades were 'much annoyed' by the French and experienced the chaos when the working parties changed over:

'The working-party was retiring to make way for the relief, and the last man stood by my side waiting his turn to pass out, (alternately) and hesitating to allow me to precede him, I desired him to pass, as I was not going; at that instant, a cannon shot (lobbed, according to the soldiers' phrase) fell upon him, and tore out his intestines entire, from his right breast to his left hip, and they hung against his thighs and legs as an apron – instantly he lost his balance and fell.'

MacCarthy called over a corporal and two other men to bury the man and, after fixing a shovel at the spot, he sat down with two engineers to watch the shells which were being thrown at the works. At that moment one of the men shouted:

'A shell is coming here, sir. I looked up, and beheld it approaching me like a cricket ball to be caught; it travelled so rapidly that we had only time to run a few paces, and crouch, when it entered the spot on which I had been sitting, and exploding, destroyed all our night's work.'

33

The British troops working in the trenches suffered great losses by these exploding shells. The trench works barely shielded the men from round shot but little or no protection was offered against these shells which often did great damage. Immediately such a shell fell every man threw himself flat against the ground until it exploded. Falling splinters were another great danger as these chunks of metal descended with 'great violence' and were capable of inflicting the most fearsome wounds.

Some Portuguese artillerymen had posted lookouts to watch the French guns and to shout a warning whenever a shell was coming. They would shout 'bomba, balla, balla, bomba,' and would duck until the danger passed, but on seeing a general salvo from all the guns they would scream 'Jesus, todos! todas!' which meant 'everything'.

Edward Costello had a curious experience one night whilst digging in the trenches. He was working with a man named Brooks, who was soon to be killed under unusual circumstances:

'Brooks, several days before his death, dreamt he saw the body of a rifleman without a head; this apparition appeared three or four nights successively in his dreams. Some days after we had taken one of the forts from the enemy, our battalion was relieved in the trenches. On this occasion, as was very customary with some of us, Brooks, another man named Tracey, and myself, jumped out of the trench, exposing ourselves to a fire from the walls of the town while we ran to the next parallel. In executing this feat I was a little ahead of my comrades, when I heard the rush of a cannon-ball, and feeling my jacket splashed by something, as soon as I had jumped into the next parallel, or trench, I turned and beheld the body of Brooks headless, which actually stood quivering with life for a few seconds before it fell. His dream, poor fellow, had singularly augured the conclusion of his own career. The shot had smashed and carried away the whole of his head, bespattering my jacket with the brains, while Tracey was materially injured by having a splinter of the skull driven deep through the skin behind his ear.'

The bad weather continued and the work in the trenches was slowed down by continuous flooding, and because of the flat level of the land it was difficult to drain away the water. By March 20 the parallel had been extended to the left across the Seville road and batteries 4, 5, and 6 were commenced. These batteries were situated in the rear of the parallel because it might prove too difficult for the guns to cross the soft ground which lay in front. Also, the batteries were within only 300 yards of the San Roque and the parallel, which now measured 1,800 yards in length, was guarded by only 1,400 men and it was feared that a sortie might be made in order to rush and spike the guns.

34

On 21 March the French placed two field guns on the right bank of the Guadiana, near the fort San Christobal, in order to enfilade the parallel but a few riflemen were posted on the bank opposite and caused them to withdraw, without doing much damage to it. During the night, however, Phillipon had thrown up a cover for these field pieces and soon after daylight on 22 March the French opened up a rather destructive fire, the shots pitching into the trenches throughout the whole day. Consequently orders were sent out to Lieutenant General Leith, commanding the 5th Division, to march and invest Badajoz from that side of the Guadiana.

That afternoon fell 'one of the heaviest showers imaginable'. The rain filled the trenches and the flood of the Guadiana ran the pontoon bridge underwater, sinking twelve of the floats, and broke the tackle of the flying bridge. All supplies for the army, provisions and ammunition were stranded on the right bank and for a while it was seriously thought that it might be necessary to retire, whilst in the trenches the earth lost all consistency and was impossible to get into any sort of shape. Much to Wellington's relief, however, the weather cleared on 23 March, the rivers subsided and a new pontoon bridge was formed from some local Portuguese craft and communications between the two banks were restored.

Work resumed and entrenchments were made opposite the castle when suddenly, at about three o'clock, as if to confirm Kincaid's views as to which side the elements had adopted, the rain again fell in torrents, filling the trenches once more and the earth, 'saturated with water, fell away, the works everywhere crumbled, and the attack was entirely suspended.' It was said afterwards that these two days were perhaps two of the most dreadful recorded in the annals of sieges. The French themselves had not been idle. In front of bastions nos. 8 and 9 they had constructed a retrenchment on the mass of earth which the Spaniards had originally thrown up in order to construct a ravelin to cover the curtain. They had also begun a communication from La Trinidad to the San Roque which, by its advanced position, might take the British attacks in the rear. Normally a work like this would be made from earth, but on this occasion, it's great length requiring too much labour, it was built partly of canvas which extended along the side of the road and was supported by poles like a curtain. The French troops passed behind this without being seen, 'to the astonishment of the English marksmen'.

They continued to strengthen the dam at the San Roque in order to retain the inundation which the British wanted to destroy and finally new platforms were laid in the castle, and embrasures cut in which were placed additional 24-pounders which were to be used to fire at the British batteries in the trenches.

From time to time Wellington would visit the trenches to see how the work progressed. MacCarthy was busy laying sandbags when the Commander-in-chief appeared with another officer:

'. . . gently walking in the trenches, where shot and shell were flying, as tranquilly as if strolling on his own lawn in England, and on approaching the medical officers, they made their obeisance and offered their glasses, one of which his lordship politely received, and also placed in the same scallop: at that instant the besieged (perhaps seeing cocked hats) fired the gun, the shot hummed as it passed over Lord Wellington's head, he smiled, but made his inspection, and returned the glass.'

Costello also saw Wellington in the trenches. He and another man, Crawley, were working in the trenches when a shell fell close to them. Crawley threw himself to the ground in order to protect himself which greatly amused Costello who intended to throw a piece onto his head to make him believe he had been wounded. At that instant another live shell fell nearby:

'. . . and on the smoke dispersing, who should I behold but the Duke himself, crouched down, his head half averted, dryly smiling at Crawley and me. Shot and shell pay no respect to persons, but the enemy did, as they seemed awake to the near vicinity of His Grace, and poured in shells, grape, and cannister, with agility, whenever he came amongst us.'

The French artillery continued to cause havoc amongst the besiegers with many a soldier meeting an unpleasant end. Cooney, a soldier with the Connaught Rangers, was concerned for his good looks after receiving a scratch on the face from a splinter:

'Whilst he was in the midst of his lamentations, a round shot struck his head and carried it off his shoulders.'

Captain Mulcaster of the Engineers, 'while standing on a rising ground, in front of battery no. 1, a 24-pound round shot struck him in the neck, and carried away his head and part of his back and shoulders. The headless trunk was knocked several yards from the spot'. Major Thomson, of the Rifles, was struck by a musket ball which passed through his brain, killing him on the spot.

Nearby, a man named North met his death in an unusual manner:

'He was struck in the cheek by a round shot; the under part of his face and portion of his throat were carried away leaving the upper part perfect, which hung down in a hideous flap, like a deformed mask.'

North was taken to hospital, but after surviving for two days he died 'after a violent effort of nature to sustain life'.

On the afternoon of 24 March Leith's 5th Division arrived on the right bank of the Guadiana and invested the town from that side. At the same time the preparations for the assault on La Picurina had reached a head. The batteries had been armed with ten 24-pounders, eleven 18-pounders and seven 5½inch howitzers, and the marksmen in the trenches kept up such a galling fire on the lunette that no French soldier dare look over the parapet. The fort was strong and a hard struggle was expected. The scarp varied from 13–16½ feet and was cut on very hard soil. Although the ditch did not have a revetted counterscarp there was a palisaded covered way all around it and the gorge was closed with a single row of palisades, the ditch had been deepened to augment the height of the scarp and the French had strenghened the gorge with a second row of palisades with a ditch before them. At the salient angle they had cut a counterscarp out of the rock and had established six small galleries, perpendicularly to the faces of the lunette which were joined together to bring a reverse fire to flank the ditches and which could not be seen from any point. Small mines were placed beneath the glacis and the ramparts were supplied with a large number of loaded shells and barrels of explosives which would be hurled down amongst the British as they attacked. The fort was garrisoned by a total of 200 men from the battalions in the town under the command of Colonel Gaspard Thierry and 200 extra muskets were placed loaded along the parapets in order that the garrison could fire several pieces.

On the dawn of 25 March the two batteries facing La Picurina were unmasked at 150 yards from the walls and at about ten o'clock they opened up a heavy fire which was returned by the guns from inside the fort itself and from the guns inside Badajoz. The parapet of La Picurina was about twelve feet thick and crumbled at each discharge from the British guns and was severely damaged, particularly at the salient angle, although this was repaired in the evening with fascines and woolpacks.

Much of the defences remained intact, however, including the three rows of palisades which still stood. The galleries for the reverse fire had been completed and the mines placed in position. Despite this the French still needed a day or so in which to get the fort into a sufficient state of defence to withstand any major assault. The British had been informed of the state of the defences by a Spanish deserter and after examining the effect of the bombardment Wellington ordered that La Picurina be stormed after dark.

The orders for the assault were given by Major-General Kempt who was in command in the trenches that afternoon. The attack would be made by 500 men of the 3rd and Light Divisions, formed into three detachments; the right, consisting of 200 men under the command of Major Shaw of the 74th; the centre, consisting of 100 men under the command of Captain Powis of the 83rd; and the remainder to form on the left under Major Rudd of the 77th. Each detachment would be preceded by the engineers Holloway, Stanway and Gipps, along with six carpenters with cutting tools, six miners with crow-bars, and twelve sappers carrying hatchets, axes and ladders.

The plan was as follows: the left detachment, led by Lieutenant Stanway, was to attack the right flank of La Picurina and try to force their way in at the gorge. The right detachment, led by Lieutenant Gipps, was to move against the communication between the fort and the town and was to leave 100 men there to prevent any reinforcements from the town from interfering. The detachment led by Captain Holloway was to prevent any of the garrison from escaping and was to give assistance to the other two detachments should they need it.

At half past seven the storming party assembled in the trenches and they were given their orders. All waited anxiously for the signal for the attack which was to be the firing of a solitary gun from battery no. 4.

Grattan sets the scene:

'The evening was settled and calm: no rain had fallen since 23 March; the rustling of a leaf may be heard; and the silence of the moment was uninterrupted, except by the French sentinels as they challenged while pacing the battlements of the outwork; the answers of their comrades, although in a lower tone of voice, were distinguishable. "Tout va bien dans le fort Picurina," was heard by the very men who awaited the signal from a gun to prove that the repouse, although true to the letter might soon be falsified.'

At about nine o'clock the three detachments sprang out of the trenches and moved quickly towards the glacis. The night was unusually dark, which favoured the British, but the noise which they inevitably made warned the already alert French and soon the fort, which before had seemed black and silent, now poured a stream of musket fire into the on-rushing columns. About 100 men fell even before they had reached the fort and those that did were denied entry by the violent musketry and by the thickness of the palisades which stood firmly in the ground. The sappers began hacking at these with their crow bars and hatchets but with little success.

Meanwhile, the Forlorn Hope had flung their ladders into the ditch and placed them against the wall, but most of the ladders were too short and did not reach the top of the parapet and the men, unable to advance, and unwilling to retire, became confused and crowded in, whilst each volley from the French defenders swept away scores of them.

'The carnage became terrible,' wrote Napier, 'the guns of Badajoz and of the castle now opened, the guard of the trenches replied with musketry,

British working parties in the forward trenches are set upon by French soldiers making a sortie.

rockets were thrown up by the besieged and the shrill sound of alarm bells, mixed with the shouts of the combatants, increased the tumult. Still the Picurina sent out streams of fire by the light of which dark figures were seen furiously struggling on the ramparts.'

By now more than two-thirds of the British troops had become casualties. The situation was desperate. Major Shaw, commander of one of the detachments, turned to his next senior officer, Oates, of the 88th, and asked him what they were to do, but at that moment Shaw was hit by a bullet and fell covered with blood. Oates now took command and he saw that although the ladders were too short to scale the walls they were long enough to cross the ditch. He immediately ordered three ladders to be thrown across the ditch and in this way a sort of bridge was formed, over which he and his men crossed, and after forcing their way through a hastily blocked up embrasure they gained entry into the fort. Oates and his party were met by a number of guards, one of whom discharged his musket, wounding Oates in the thigh. At the sight of their commanding

39

officer 'weltering in his blood', the already excited British lost all self-control and every guard was put to death.

Meanwhile, the axe-men, 'compassing the fort like prowling wolves', were trying to hack their way in at the rear.

'The soldiers walked round the fort,' wrote John Cooke, 'prying into all corners, and got upon the gate, which they broke down, and then entered, bayonets in advance. The French grenadiers would not give in – a desperate bayonetting took place and much blood was spilt . . . the struggle continued with hard fighting inside and outside the fort. The enemy wished to vie with their comrades who had defended the fort San Christobal at the former siege. Victory was for some minutes doubtful; at length the fort was our own, and the reinforcements were beat back into the town.'

Captain Powis' detachment had entered the fort at the salient angle at a point at which the palisades had been damaged by artillery fire, and as soon as the attack at this point had succeeded, La Picurina fell into British hands. Governor Phillipon had selected a battalion of the 103rd Regiment to counter-attack from the San Roque but it was too late. They met a strong body of British troops under Captain Lindsay, of the 88th, and such was the heavy fire from La Picurina, now in British hands, and from the troops posted near the communication with the town, that they fled in disorder back into the town.

About a hundred men of the garrison were killed or wounded and sixty were taken prisoners, including Colonel Thierry. Many French troops had tried to escape by crossing the trestle bridge connecting with the town but it was half demolished and in the panic many of them were drowned. Only one officer and thirty men of the Hessian Regiment managed to escape back to the town.

As soon as it became clear that La Picurina had fallen Phillipon ordered his artillery to commence a heavy fire on the fort to prevent the British from securing a lodgment in it. Despite the fire from the French guns, which did not cease until long after midnight, a communication was formed into the work by a ramp at the salient angle which was connected to the first parallel and supported on the left by a part of the second parallel which extended to the inundation.

The British casualties sustained in the assault on La Picurina were four officers and fifty men killed and 250 men wounded, out of a total of a little over 500 men engaged. Amongst the wounded officers were Majors Rudd and Shaw and Captain Powis, all of whom had led a detachment to the assault, and all three of the guides, Lieutenants Gipps and Stanway and Captain Holloway. Captain Powis later died of his wounds.

Governor Phillipon and General Veiland were both greatly annoyed by the weak resistance put up by the garrison of La Picurina as they had hoped that the fort might be able to hold out for about five or six days. They were amazed at their inability and failure to make use of the many loaded shells and explosives that had been placed around the parapets and on the glacis. There had been two successful defences made the previous year by the defenders of the San Christobal, when hand grenades and loaded shells were 'thrown in showers' amongst the British and it was hoped that the defenders of La Picurina might do likewise. In his journal of the siege, Lamare wrote that Captain Marcillac, who commanded the fort's artillery, had been wounded earlier during the day and had been replaced by a less capable and brave officer and he believed that had Marcillac been on duty that day the British would have been repulsed.

Now Phillipon, well aware of the dangerous situation in which he was placed, tried to stir the courage of his men by reminding them they would be well advised to make a long and vigorous resistance, for it was better to die for the glory of France than to be held captive aboard one of the English prison ships. Lamare wrote 'the whole world is acquainted with the barbarity with which the English treated their prisoners. France will never forget the sufferings which her soldiers endured aboard the Hulks.'

Meanwhile, Wellington had moved three battalions of reserves forward to occupy the fort and work was begun on the lodgments, continuing through the night. But by daylight on 26 March the fire from the guns in Badajoz had became so heavy that no troops could remain inside the redoubt which was overwhelmed by fire, and the works inside destroyed.

Before nightfall, however, the engineers had completed a new lodgment on the flanks and a second parallel was opened up along the whole length of the fort. The British batteries on the right of La Picurina had begun to return the fire of the French guns but with little apparent effect. One of the British guns was put out of action and the fire from the inexperienced Portuguese gunners was likewise ineffectual.

The French guns kept up a continual barrage throughout the day and Lamare estimated that along with a vast quantity of shells fired 12,000lbs of powder were used, which, added to the 70,000lbs of powder used since the siege began, amounted to about half the original quantity the French had provided themselves with. In view of this they were forced to slacken their fire in order to spare ammunition.

During the night of 26-7 March the British engineers began tracing out the ground for the batteries to be used to breach the bastions in Badajoz. No. 7 battery consisted of twelve 24-pounders and was to breach the right face of La Trinidad bastion, while no. 9 battery consisted of eight 18-pounders and was to breach the left face of the Santa Maria bastion. A third battery, no. 10, contained four 24-pounder iron howitzers and would enfilade the ditch in front of the breaches to prevent the enemy from working there.

By now Phillipon could see the true line of attack and sent out working parties to raise the counterguard of La Trinidad bastion and the unfinished ravelin covering that front. By morning of 27 March these works had been completed and strengthened with gabions and sandbags and the French infantry lining them opened up a galling fire upon the workmen constructing the breaking batteries. Both sides' artillery were in action against each other and two British guns were knocked out.

By the morning of 28 March the British had pushed forward a zig-zag from their parallel in order to approach the lunette San Roque. The idea was to try and destroy the dam which held the water in the inundation of the Rivellas, making it easier for themselves to cross. The Talavera road was made of hard rock, however, and proved difficult to cut without making loud noises and in the bright moonlight earlier the workmen were exposed to the French sentries, some casualties being sustained. The sap was continued throughout the day in spite of one particularly daring French soldier who, Lamare tells us, had crept out in the dark and had placed the tracing string which marked the direction of the sap into line with the fire from the French guns in the castle. The British workmen suffered some casualties before the trick was discovered.

Towards nightfall a new breaching battery had been traced out on the site of La Picurina to fire against the flank of the Santa Maria bastion and a battery of 24-pounders, to be used against the San Roque, was also unmasked. The second parallel was cut across the Talavera road and a trench was dug in front of the batteries for the riflemen to use.

The British had continued their sap on the right bank as far as a small knoll opposite the Tête du Pont. These works were separated from the town by the river and the French were in no way affected by them. Phillipon thought it proper, however, that a sortie be made against them. The task was entrusted to 400 men of the 9th Light Infantry who were under the command of chief of battalion Billion. They marched quickly out through the gates and across the Tête du Pont and against the workmen in the trenches, but this time the British had brought forward a large part of their force and the French were forced to withdraw after inflicting little damage. The officer who had proposed the sortie, Lieutenant Duhamel, was killed as were a few of the 9th, whilst the besiegers suffered no casualties.

The next day the French lost another much respected officer, Truilhier, of the Engineers, who received a mortal wound in the head whilst working in the trenches. The officer had distinguished himself at the defence of Almeida where he blew up the

42

fortifications. He had asked to be allowed to have the honour of helping defend Badajoz and his death was mourned by the whole garrison.

On the afternoon of 30 March, Grattan found himself working with about thirty other men, covering a magazine with boards and sandbags, when suddenly, at about three o'clock, a shell rolled into it and exploded:

'destroying all that side of the magazine, and hurling the planks, which were but in part secured on top, together with the men that were upon them, into the air, causing us a great loss of lives and labour, but fortunately the great store of powder which was inside escaped. The planks were shivered to pieces and the brave fellows who occupied them, either blown into atoms or so dreadfully wounded as to cause their immediate death; some had their uniform burnt to a cinder while others were coiled up in a heap without the vestige of anything left to denote that they were human beings.'

While the siege wore on Soult was marching to unite with the French armies under Drouet and Daricau. Remembering the fine defence of Badajoz made by Phillipon the previous year and aware of the efficient state of the defences he was convinced that the town was in no immediate danger and that it could hold out for a while yet. As late as 1 April he was still at Seville, nine days' march away, whilst Daricau and Drouet had been in the district of La Llerena in order to keep in touch with Marmont, but Graham and Hill had forced them both back by the Cordova roads into the Morena. Instead of trying to push on to help Soult attempt to relieve Badajoz, Marmont had allowed himself to become side-tracked and had spent two precious days fighting the Portuguese, and after recrossing the Agueda he left Soult and Badajoz to their fates.

The Spanish army had also been busy delaying the French. In February General Montes had defeated Maransin on the Guadajore river, forcing him into Malaga. Following this, the whole Spanish army assembled in the Ronda hills with the intention of attacking Seville. This forced Soult to send troops to Malaga and this cost precious days and further delayed his march on Badajoz. On 30 March Soult's advance was confirmed and to cover the British, Leith's 5th Division crossed the Guadiana, with Power's Portuguese Brigade continuing the investment from the right bank.

Inside Badajoz the French worked hard on the interior retrenchments of the two bastions which were to be attacked. A separate retrenchment was also formed in the rear by making use of the gardens and demolished houses behind. The streets were cut across with ditches and traverses and to the last moment they were perfecting these works.

On the last day of March the two breaching batteries, armed with twenty-six heavy guns, opened fire against the right face of La

The walls of the Santa Maria bastion today. The neatly laid gardens replace what was once the ditch.

Trinidad bastion and the flank of the Santa Maria bastion. The other batteries sent shells and case shot into the French works. The French replied vigorously, firing at least 5,000 cannon balls during the day as well as a heavy musket fire which continued into the night. Lamare described the effects of the guns:

'Before night there was a good deal of rubbish at the foot of the wall which working parties and sappers went to clear. Our brave troops always executed these operations with the greatest courage, remaining exposed for four or five hours to grape shot and the projectiles of every description which the enemy directed upon the point. The town also suffered much; desolation was general amongst its inhabitants; the greatest number terror-struck sought refuge in the cellars, and in the churches, which they imagined to be bomb proof but where many were killed under their frail protection. The garrison had no casemates whatsoever, nor even the smallest shelter from blinds; nevertheless our loss in killed and wounded from 16 March to the present moment did not exceed 700 men.'

During the night, two British officers with some sappers 'gliding behind', made an attempt to destroy the dam at the San Roque to lower the waters which filled the inundation. The French sentinels were gagged and powder barrels placed against the dam, but the explosion failed to destroy it and the inundation remained. The sap in front of the San Roque made little progress too. The French sent out a party of infantry on a reinforced raft which floated across the inundation and opened fire on the workmen. The raft faced the British lines and was raised by light poles to a height of four feet. It was padded and could withstand musketry and could support up to forty men. Other troops passed behind the cloth communication from a Trinidad gate and opened fire from there. To counter these moves several hundred riflemen were positioned to open fire upon the raft and the French infantry as soon as they were seen.

1 April saw the British guns blasting away at La Trinidad bastion. The parapet of the right face as well as that of the right face of the Santa Maria bastion was almost completely destroyed. A new parapet was constructed behind from sandbags and bales of cotton-wool which were replaced as fast as the cannon shots carried them away. By now the French artillery began to slacken. In spite of the care which they had taken to preserve their powder the supply had dwindled and consumption was now fixed at 6,500lbs per day. This meant that they had only enough powder to last until 9 April. Shells and case shot were also in short supply. But despite these shortages and the desperate position they were in, the garrison showed no signs of disillusion. Their spirits were high. They were quite confident of being able to repulse several assaults and Phillipon neglected nothing that could maintain this spirit.

The British bombardment continued throughout 2 April and again an attempt was made to blow up the dam, but once again they were driven off by the guard of the San Roque under Captain Saintourners, of the 58th Regiment.

In the trenches, George Simmons, of the Rifles, lay in wait to pick off any unwary gunners in the town, with a good deal of success:

'I was with a party of men behind the advanced sap, and had an opportunity of doing some mischief. Three or four heavy cannon that the enemy were working were doing frightful execution amongst our artillerymen in the advanced batteries. I selected several good shots and fired into the embrasures. In half an hour I found the guns did not go off so frequently as before I commenced this practice, and soon after, gabions were stuffed into each embrasure to prevent our rifle balls from entering. They then withdrew them to fire, which was my signal for firing steadily at the embrasures. The gabions were replaced without firing the shot. I was so delighted with the good practice I was making against Johnny that I kept it up from daylight till dark with forty prime fellows as ever pulled trigger. These guns were literally silenced. A French officer (I suppose a marksman), who hid himself in some long grass, first placed his cocked hat some little distance from him for us to fire at. Several of his men handed him loaded muskets in order that he might fire more frequently. I was leaning half over the trench watching his movements. I observed his head, and being exceedingly anxious that the man who was going to fire should

View from the ramparts of the Castle. The right of the British lines was situated in the distance beyond the present course of the Rivellas which can easily be discerned running across the centre of the picture.

see him, I directed him to lay his rifle over my left shoulder as a more elevated rest for him. He fired. Through my eagerness, I had entirely overlooked his pan, so that it was in close contact with my left ear; and a pretty example it made of it and the side of my head, which was singed and the ear cut and burnt. The poor fellow was very sorry for the accident. We soon put the Frenchman out of that. He left his cocked hat, which remained until dark, so that we had either killed or wounded him. My friends in camp jocked me a good deal the next morning, observing, "Pray, what's the matter with your ear? How did the injury happen?" and so on. Weather for some days good.'

On 3 April, another battery opened fire against La Trinidad. The guns of this battery were to ricochet their shots off the face battered in the breach and into the retrenchments behind to prevent the French from working there. Their guns could not reply in strength now, owing to their desire to preserve their ammunition, but to compensate for this their best marksmen were placed in the covered ways and at loop holes and rifle pits and from there they opened up a galling fire at the British gunners, causing many casualties. There was no slacking from the guns however:

'Death was dealt in every direction amongst us,' wrote Lamare, 'the ramparts were crumbling to pieces, the breaches becoming practicable, the efforts which the workmen made nightly to clear them, were ineffectual. In this state of things the Council of defence was assembled in order to make the last arrangements.'

46

It was at this meeting that Phillipon decided which troops were to defend the breaches. The task was entrusted to 700 men from the artillery and engineers together with the Grenadiers and the Light Infantry. Phillipon gave over the command of this important and perilous position to Barbot, of the 88th Regiment, and Maistre of the Hessian Regiment. Lurat, of the 103rd, was in command of a battalion placed in reserve in a retrenchment behind the breaches. These defensive works increased as the siege pressed on and Phillipon and General Veiland inspected them daily, encouraging the men. Whilst at these works in the breaches Phillipon received a slight wound in the shoulder, whilst Veiland and two of his aides escaped injury when some case shot passed through their uniforms.

Lamare again:

'On 4 April we continued our preparations for sustaining the assault; the artillery had posted their men at the guns in the flanks of the bastions, loaded with grape shot. At about ten o'clock in the morning a strong column of the enemy's infantry arrived by the Elvas road, on the left bank of the river, and formed on the Albuera road. We also observed a long train of waggons loaded with scaling ladders and all the preparations which announced an approaching assault.'

Throughout 5 April, thirty-eight British guns hammered away at the bastions of La Trinidad and Santa Maria, and it was reported to Wellington that the breaches would be practicable by sunset. As he was inspecting the breaches Wellington was informed that Soult had reached Llerena the previous day. The critical point in the siege had now arrived. Wellington had no wish to take Badajoz by storm and wanted more time perhaps even to force the garrison to surrender. But on hearing the news that Soult was closing in he had no choice but to order the assault to be made later that evening.

As the British troops awaited the appointed hour their spirits rose and the atmosphere was charged with expectancy.

'The spirits of the soldiers, which no fatigues could dampen, rose to a frightful height,' wrote Grattan, 'I say frightful because it was not of that sort which alone denoted exultation at the prospect of an exploit which was about to hold them up to the admiration of the world, there was a certain something in their bearing that told plainly they had suffered fatigues, which, though they did not complain of, and had seen their comrades slain while fighting beside them without repining – they smarted under the one, and felt acutely for the other, yet smothered both so long as their bodies and minds were employed; now, however, that they had a momentary licence to think, every fine feeling vanished and plunder and revenge took their place...In a word, the capture of Badajoz had long been their idol; many causes led to this wish on their part; the two previous unsuccessful sieges, and the failure of the attack against San Christobal in the latter; but above all, the well known hostility of its inhabitants to the British army, and perhaps might be added, a desire for plunder which the sacking of Rodrigo had given them a taste for. Badajoz was, therefore, denounced as a place to be made example of; and most unquestionably no city, Jerusalem exempted, was ever more strictly visited to the letter than was this ill-fated town.'

The British troops prepared themselves for the assault which they thought, from the appearance of the breaches, was to take place that night. Men gave what little effects they had to their friends and all sorts of arrangements were made between the men. They stood around in groups and a little light rain fell, but it could not dampen their spirits. A quiet calm now set in and no emotion was to be seen, except for a 'tiger-like expression of anxiety to seize upon their prey, which was considered within their grasp'.

At about four o'clock, however, a group of officers arrived in the camp with a report that Wellington had countermanded his original order and that the assault was now postponed. It seemed that the French had accumulated all manner of deadly obstacles in the breaches and Colonel Fletcher, after having recovered from his wound, had made an inspection of them and had recommended a third breach be made in the curtain between the two breached bastions.

At this news the men became angry and dejected, violence broke out and the engineers were roundly abused. But after they had overcome their disappointment they realised that the third breach must be necessary to their success or else Wellington would not have allowed it.

As a precautionary measure against Soult's advance Leith's 5th Division was brought round to the Sierro del Viento, about a mile and a quarter to the south-west of Badajoz, whilst Hill, after breaking down the bridge at Merida, withdrew to Talavera de Real, twelve miles away. In case Soult approached any nearer Wellington arranged that while two divisions remained in the trenches, the rest of the army would march to Albuera, and if necessary give battle.

On the morning of 6 April the fourteen howitzers which had been moved to the right of the first parallel during the night opened fire on the curtain between the Trinidad and the Santa Maria, and by four o'clock in the afternoon a practicable breach had been blasted through. Every gun was now turned on the town's defences and Wellington gave the order for the place to be stormed at half past seven that evening. However, it proved impossible to complete the preparations and the hour of attack was put back to ten. This allowed the French to shore up the defences again, and because of an oversight the British had neglected to destroy the counterscarp. This should have been blown into the ditch, enabling the storming columns to climb over the rubble and rush into the breaches. Instead of this they would have to jump into the ditch, form up, and then make the assault from there. The French had taken advantage of this and had raised the earthen counterguards and retrenchments to cover the curtain between the bastions of La Trinidad and Santa Maria, and between the San Pedro and the San Antonio.

At the foot of the counterscarp Phillipon had dug a ditch which now raised its height to sixteen feet. In this ditch Wellington had planned to form his troops, but the French, unseen by the besiegers, had filled it with water and this was to cause the British much trouble. In the breaches, were placed all sorts of obstacles necessary for a stiff defence. Along all of the accessible places the French had placed the savage chevaux-de-frise, made from razor-sharp cavalry sabres; fascines, sandbags and woolpacks took the place of fallen ramparts, and the slopes of the breaches were covered with planks studded with twelve-inch spikes, and chained to the ground. Explosives were taken from the artillery stores and powder barrels were placed ready to be rolled down into the ditch to explode amongst the British.

All sorts of shells and combustibles were laid along the parapets ready for use and each man was armed with three muskets. Lieutenant de Ruffey, of the 58th Regiment, had even proposed to place a boat at the salient angle of La Trinidad bastion, in order to enfilade the assaulting troops on the glacis. The idea was seized upon and the boat placed in position. Finally, at the foot of the counterscarp, immediately in front of the breaches, were arranged sixty fourteen-inch shells, at about four yards apart, in a circle, and were covered with earth. Powder hoses, placed between tubes, were arranged as 'mine tubes' and were designed to act as fuses and Lieutenant Maillet of the Miners was charged with detonating them.

When all was ready the gallant Phillipon, still suffering from the slight wound received on 3 April, moved amongst his men, reminding them of their duty and of the need to prolong the defence everywhere and by every means, and 'to make the enemy pay with the blood of his best soldiers the capture of a fortress which it appeared he must at last take'.

Wellington ordered the assault to begin at ten o'clock. Picton's 3rd Division were to move out from the right of the first parallel shortly before ten o'clock. They were to cross the Rivellas and take the castle by escalade.

The 4th Division, under Colville, leaving behind a covering party in the trenches, were to storm the breach of La Trinidad, and Barnard's Light Division the breach in the Santa Maria. The Light Division were to place a hundred men in the quarries near the covered way of the Santa Maria to keep down the fire from the defenders placed there, and firing parties would be spread along the glacis to keep down the enemy's fire whilst the storming parties rushed on to the breaches.

The advance parties of each Division would consist of 500 men, carrying with them twelve ladders, and the men of the Forlorn Hope were to carry large sacks of grass which were to be thrown into the ditches to break the fall of the troops jumping into it.

On the left, Leith was to make a false attack on the Pardaleras and if possible an attack by escalade on the San Vincente bastion. Finally, a detachment from the guard in the trenches under Major Wilson, of the 48th, were to storm the San Roque, whilst General Power's Portuguese brigade on the right of the Guadiana were to make a false attack on the San Christobal.

The hour had been set, the orders given. This time there would be no postponement and the soldiers settled down to wait. As on the previous day the spirits of the troops were high.

'In proportion as the grand crisis approached, the anxiety of the soldiers increased,' wrote Kincaid, 'not on any account of any doubt or dread as to the result, but for fear that the place be surrendered without standing an

The Defence of Badajoz. Phillipon and his men swear to fight till the end. There were no eagles in the town despite the one shown in the picture.

assault, for, singular as it may appear, although there was a certainty of about one man out of every three being knocked down, there were perhaps not three men in the three divisions who would not rather have braved all the chances than receive it tamely from the hands of the enemy. So great was the rage for passports into eternity, in any battalion, on that occasion, that even the officers' servants insisted on taking their place in the ranks, and I was obliged to leave my baggage in charge of a man who had been wounded some days before.'

Bugler William Green, of the Rifle Brigade, bears out this testament:

'Our bugle major made us cast lots which two of us should go on this momentous errand; the lot fell on me and another lad. But one of our buglers who had been on the Forlorn Hope at Ciudad Rodrigo offered the bugle major two dollars to let him go in my stead. On my being apprised of

52

it, he came to me, and said "West will go on the Forlorn Hope instead of you." I said "I shall go where my duty calls me." He threatened to confine me to the guard tent. I went to the adjutant, and reported him; the adjutant sent for him, and said, "So you are in the habit of taking bribes;" and told him he would take the stripes off his arm if he did the like again! He then asked me if I wished to go? I said "Yes, sir." He said "Very good," and dismissed me. Those who composed this Forlorn Hope were free from duty that day, so I went to the river, and had a good bathe; I thought I would have a clean skin whether killed or wounded, for all who go on this errand expect one or the other.'

MacCarthy wrote:

'To describe the hilarity of the officers and soldiers, individually preparing for a premeditated attack, would be extremely difficult – the officers with servants carefully packing their portmanteaus, and the soldiers in like manner packing their knapsacks, to leave in their encampments secure, so as to be readily found on their return – without for one moment considering the certainty of their not returning; the men fixing their best flints in their muskets, and all forming in column, with the utmost alacrity, to march to the assault...'

By five o'clock on the afternoon of 6 April, all the ladders had been issued and the preparations completed. The time given for the troops to assemble was eight o'clock and as the night closed in and each hour passed, longer than the one before it, the troops waited. At eight o'clock the bell of the clock in the town was heard throughout the silent British lines as it tolled the hour for the battalions to move forward to their assembly points, and after piling arms the men settled down once again to wait for the signal to assault Badajoz.

4

The Storm

The night of 6 April was dry and cloudy, not a star could be seen to shine anywhere in the sky. A thick dusky vapour had risen from the Rivellas and the Guadiana, and hung like a veil between the two forces. Everything was still and nothing could be heard except the gentle rippling of the rivers and the croaking of the frogs. The musket and artillery fire which had been incessant for the past weeks 'now ceased as if by mutual consent, and a deathlike silence of nearly an hour preceded the awful scene of carnage'. As they waited in silence the British troops could hear the night watch within the town's walls crying 'all's well in Badajoz'. The siege had taken its toll of the troops and by now they looked anything but British soldiers. They had discarded their knapsacks, their shirts were unbuttoned, many were barefoot and had tucked their trousers in at the knees. Their uniforms were in tatters and their faces were dirty, bronzed and bearded. They were barely recognisable as British troops but 'their self-confidence...gave them the appearance of what they, in reality, were – an invincible host'.

At twenty minutes to ten the silence was broken by the rattle of musket fire from the San Roque. The British troops in the sap had opened fire on the two faces of the lunette while the storming party moved against the rear and planted their ladders against the ramparts. They met with little resistance and the lunette was taken. Major Wilson, of the 48th, was in command of 300 men ordered to take the San Roque; Lieutenant Robert Knowles, of the 7th Fusiliers, was one of them.

'When the 3rd Division advanced to commence their attack upon the castle we advanced to the Raveline, and after considerable difficulty we succeeded in placing one ladder against the wall, about twenty-four feet high. A Corporal of mine was the first to mount it, and he was killed at the top of it. I was the third or fourth, and when in the act of leaping off the wall into the Fort I was knocked down by a discharge from the enemy, the handle of my sabre broke into a hundred pieces, my hand disabled, and at the same time I received a very severe bruise on my side, and a slight wound, a piece of lead (having penetrated through my haversack, which was nearly filled with bread, meat, and a small stone brandy-bottle for use in the trenches during the night) lodged upon one side of my ribs, but without doing any serious injury. I recovered myself as soon as possible, and by the time seven or eight of my brave fellows had got into the fort, I

Richard Simkin's somewhat fanciful impression of the scaling of the walls at Badajoz, which were a good deal higher than depicted here.

charged along the ramparts, killing or destroying all who opposed us. I armed myself with the first Frenchman's firelock I met with, and carried it as well as I was able under my arm. The greater part of my party having joined me, we charged into the Fort, when they all cried out "prisoners".'

55

The Castle walls of Badajoz today, as seen from the direction of the approach of the 3rd Division.

With the San Roque taken, Knowles sat himself down on a wall and had a fine view of the different attacks on the town. Shortly afterwards the main attack commenced.

William Green:

'We were told to go as still as possible, and every word of command was given in a whisper. I had been engaged in the field about twenty-six times, and had never got a wound; we had about a mile to go to the place of attack, so off we went with palpitating hearts. I never feared nor saw danger till this night. As I walked at the head of the column, the thought struck me very forcibly "You will be in hell before daylight!" Such a feeling of horror I had never experienced before.'

The Forlorn Hope moved forward first, followed by the storming parties, and as they moved quickly and quietly across the ground they could see the heads of the French defenders lining the ramparts. Lamare wrote:

'A very dark night favoured their approach. The columns of attack arrived on the glacis without being seen; the heads of these columns instantly leaped into the ditches and arrived at the foot of the ruins. The clinking of arms was heard; a sudden cry was raised – "there they are! there they are!" '

A remarkable aerial shot, taken from a balloon in 1914, showing the area of the breaches as they probably appeared in 1812. Sadly, this has completely changed today and what were once deadly defences are now neatly-laid gardens. (1) is the San Pedro bastion, (2) is the Trinidad bastion, breached at the point below the number 2, and (3) is the Santa Maria bastion, breached in its right flank. The curtain wall between the two bastions was also breached. The British siege guns were positioned in trenches away to the right. In the background is the Guadiana, while the course of the Rivellas can easily be followed.

The storming parties dashed forward to the edge of the ditch, placed their ladders in position and descended. The red columns of British troops came on and soon the ditch was filled with men crowding together. Suddenly a bright flame shot up exposing the columns to the watching French who had been waiting for the ditch to fill. Now they lit the fuse which would explode the mines in front of the breaches. John Spencer Cooper went in with the 7th Fusiliers:

'When our men had approached within 300 yards of the ditch, up went a fireball. This showed the crowded state of the ramparts, and the bright arms of our approaching columns. Those men who carried grass bags to fill up the ditch, and ladders for escalading the walls, were now hurried forward. Instantly the whole rampart was in a blaze; mortars, cannon, and muskets, roared and rattled unceasingly. Mines ever and anon blew up with horrid noise. To add to this horrible din, there were the sound of bugles, the rattling of drums, and the shouting of the combatants. Through a tremendous fire our men rushed to the top of the glacis, down the ladders, and up the breach. But entrance was impossible, for across the horrid gap the enemy had placed, in spite of our fire, a strong beam full of sword blades, etc, forming a chevaux-de-frise, behind which, entrenched, stood many ranks of soldiers, whose fire swept the breach from end to end. Besides, the top of the parapet was covered with shells, stones, sand bags, and logs of wood, etc, ready to be thrown into the ditch. As the breaches could not be forced, and as our men kept pouring down the ladders, the whole ditch was soon filled with a dense mass which could neither advance nor retreat. Upon these the enemy threw the missiles from the parapet, with a continuous fire of musketry and round shot. My comrade was killed while descending a ladder. Some men went further to the right, and jumped into that part of the ditch that was filled with water, and were drowned.'

Lieutenant John Cooke wrote:

'The ladders were placed in the ditch when an explosion took place at the foot of the breaches, and a burst of bright light disclosed the whole scene – the earth seemed to rock under us – what a sight! The ramparts crowded with the enemy – the French soldiers standing on the parapets – the 4th Division advancing rapidly in column of companies on a half-circle to our right, while the short-lived glare from the barrels of powder and combustibles flying into the air, gave to friends and foes a look as if bodies of troops were laughing at each other.'

The storming parties were blown to pieces with 'incredible violence' by the explosions and a blaze of musketry and grape opened up against the British troops on the glacis, sweeping them away in scores and hundreds. The Light Division stood on the edge of the ditch and 'amazed at the terrific sight' they let out a wild, deafening shout and flew down the ladders into the fiery chasm below, whilst at the same time the 4th Division came charging in, and descended like

The Storming of Badajoz. Note the chevaux-de-frise and the water.

fury. Edward Costello was one of the men detailed to carry a ladder and a grass bag:

'Three of the men carrying the ladder with me were shot dead in a breath, and its weight falling upon me, I fell backward with the grass bag on my breast. The remainder of the stormers rushed up, regardless of my cries or of those of the wounded men around me, for by this time our men were falling fast. Many in passing were shot and fell upon me so that I was actually drenched in blood.'

As the men of the 4th Division came on to attack the right hand breach they met with disaster. The leading columns jumped into that part of the ditch which the French had filled with water and about a hundred men drowned before the tragic mistake was realised, but 'the bubbles that rose to the surface,' wrote Grattan, 'were a terrible assurance of the struggles which those devoted soldiers ineffectually made to extricate each other.' By now Costello had freed himself and he made for the breach:

'I slid quickly down the ladder, but before I could recover my footing, was knocked down again by the bodies of men who were shot in attempting the

59

descent. I, however, succeeded in extricating myself from underneath the dead, and pushing to the right, to my surprise and fear I found myself up to my neck in water. Until then I was tolerably composed, but now all reflection left me, and diving through the water, being a good swimmer, I attempted to make for the breach.'

As the remainder of the 4th Division watched the bubbles rise to the surface of the water they turned left and collided with the men of the Light Division and both divisions made for the same point. Coming together opposite the unfinished ravelin, which was rough and unbroken, the two divisions mistook it for the breach and swarmed over the earthwork to attack. They were met by a blaze of musketry 'unlike anything hitherto witnessed by the oldest soldier' and were thrown back in disorder. Crowded together, confused and blinded by the flashing of the guns that wreaked havoc and destruction amongst them, the two divisions now made for the breach of the La Trinidad, which the 4th Division had originally planned to attack. Many men reached the summit but were destroyed on the chevaux-de-frise or were swept away by the hail of musket balls.

Harry Smith wrote:

'We flew down the ladders and rushed at the breach, but we were broken and carried no weight with us, although every soldier was a hero. The breach was covered by a breastwork from behind and ably defended on the top by chevaux-de-frise of sword blades, sharp as razors, chained to the ground; while the ascent to the top of the breach was covered with planks with sharp nails in them. However, devil a one did I feel at this moment. One of the officers of the Forlorn Hope, Lieutenant Taggart, of the 43rd, was hanging on my arm – a mode we adopted to help each other up; for the ascent was most difficult and steep. A Rifleman stood among the sword blades at the top of one of the chevaux-de-frise. We made a glorious rush to follow, but, alas! in vain. He was knocked over . . . I had been some seconds at the revetment of the bastion near the breach, and my red coat pockets were literally filled with chips of stones splintered by musket balls. Those not knocked down were driven back by this hail of mortality to the ladders.'

'Gallant foes,' wrote Robert Blakeney, 'laughing at death met, fought, bled and rolled upon earth; and from the very earth destruction burst, for the exploding mines cast up friend and foe together, who in burning torture clashed and shrieked in the air. Partly burned they fell back into the inundating water, continually lighted by the incessant bursting of shells. Thus assailed by opposing elements they made the horrid scene yet more horrid by shrieks uttered in wild despair vainly struggling against a watery grave with limbs convulsed and quivering from the consuming fire.'

The two divisions were now mixed together and the confusion was increased when a Portuguese brigade, which had been held in

Serrez les Ranjs. French infantry, 1812 as they probably would have appeared defending Badajoz.

reserve, came forward from the quarries to join the assault. As the men struggled to get forward, blows were exchanged and the men in front were forced forward on the points of the bayonets of those behind. The noise was deafening. The loud cheering and the sound of exploding grenades and artillery fire was joined by the roaring of the British guns in the trenches.

No impression could be made by the assailing British troops, however, and the French defenders, gaining confidence from their ability to withstand the assaults, came forward and began to let loose a violent hail of shot from their muskets. In addition to the normal charge the French had loaded their muskets with a small cylinder of wood stuck full of leaden slugs which scattered 'like hail' when fired.

Cooke again:

'Death and the most dreadful sounds encompassed us. It was a volcano! Up we went; some killed and some impaled on the bayonets of their own comrades, or hurled headlong amongst the outrageous crowd. The chevaux-de-frise looked like innumerable bayonets. When within a yard of the top my sensations were extraordinary; I felt half strangled, and fell from a blow that deprived me of sensation. I only recollect feeling a soldier pulling me out of the water, where so many men were drowned. I lost my cap, but still held my sword; on recovering, I looked towards the breach. It was shining and empty! Fire-balls were in plenty, and the French troops standing upon the walls, taunting and inviting our men to come up and try it again. What a crisis! What a military misery! Some of the finest troops in the world prostrate – humbled to the dust.'

Bell wrote:

'Slaughter, tumult and disorder continued; no command could be heard, the wounded struggling to free themselves from under the bleeding bodies of their comrades; the enemy's guns within a few yards at every fire, opening a bloody lane amongst our people who closed up, and, with shouts of terror as the lava burned them up, pressed on to destruction – officers starting forward with an heroic impulse, carried on their men to the yawning breach and glittering steel, which still continued to belch out flames of scorching death.'

William Green was in the act of throwing the grass bag which he was carrying when:

'a ball went through the thick part of my thigh, and having my bugle in my left hand, it entered my left wrist and I dropped, so I did not get into the ditch. I scarcely felt the ball go through my thigh, but when it entered my wrist, it was more like a 6-pounder than a musket-ball! It smashed the bone and cut the guides, and the blood was pouring from both wounds, I began to feel very faint. Our men were in the ditch, while the enemy had shells loaded on the top of the wall about two yards apart. As they were fired they rolled into the ditch, and when they burst, ten or twelve men were blown up in every direction! . . . The whole of the division made for the breach; and a tremendous fire was going on. I heard our bugle major sound the advance and double-quick I rolled on my back (for I had fell on my side) and repeated the sound; this was the last time I blew the bugle. As another division came past me, an officer with his sword drawn stepped up to me

The walls of the San Vincente bastion today. No trees or bushes in 1812.

and said "Desist blowing that bugle, you are drawing all the fire on my men!" I said "I was only doing my duty!" '

Green managed to get to his feet and hobble to the rear and was eventually helped to a surgeon who attended him. George Simmons, also with the Rifle Brigade wrote:

'Our storming party was soon hotly engaged. Our columns moved on under a most dreadful fire of grape, that mowed down our men like grass. We tore down the palisading and got upon the glacis. The havoc now became dreadful. My captain (Grey) was shot in the mouth. Eight or ten officers, and men innumerable, fell to rise no more. Ladders were resting against the counterscarp from within the ditch. Down these we hurried, and as fast as we got down rushed forward to the breaches, where a most frightful scene of carnage was going on. Fifty times they were stormed, and as often without effect, the French cannon sweeping the ditches with a most destructive fire. Lights were thrown amongst us from the town that burnt most brilliantly, and made us easier to be shot at. In this way we remained for a considerable time. I was in a sort of frenzy stamping one of these lights out when an officer laid hold of me, saying, "Leave it, or when the light goes out your feet will be blown to pieces, as there is a live shell connected with it." The ditch now, from the place where we entered to near the top of the breaches, was covered with dead and dying soldiers. If a man fell wounded, ten to one that he ever rose again, for the volleys of musketry and grape shot

63

that were incessantly poured amongst us made our situation too horrid for description. I had seen some fighting, but nothing like this. We remained passively here to be slaughtered, as we could do the besieged little injury from the ditch. We were ordered to leave the ditch and move away from the works.'

From the French point of view everything so far had gone well. The British had failed to make any impression on the defences and no man had got beyond the entrenchments and lived. One rifleman had crawled beneath the sword blades but he was found next morning with his head 'battered to pieces and his arms and shoulders riddled with bayonet thrusts'. The French now grew more confident and began to taunt the despairing British with loud laughter and cries of: 'why don't you come into Badajoz?'

The attacks continued, however. Costello had just climbed from the water in the ditch and he approached one of the chevaux-de-frise:

'. . . but before reaching it I received a stroke on the breast, whether from a grenade or a stone I cannot say, but down I rolled senseless, and drenched with water, and human gore . . . I endeavoured, among the dead bodies around me, to screen myself from the enemy's shot; but while I lay in this position, the fire still continued blazing over me in all its horrors, accompanied by screams, groans and shouts, and the crashing of stones and falling of timbers. I now, for the first time in many years, uttered something like a prayer.'

Young Colonel Macleod, of the 43rd, had led his men up the ruins in repeated attacks, even after one of his own men had plunged their bayonet into his back whilst falling wounded. Despite this, Macleod continued forward but was shot within a yard of the sword blades.

'Again did they attempt to pass this terrible gulf of steel and flame,' wrote Grattan, 'and again were driven back, cut down, annihilated. Hundreds of brave soldiers lay in piles upon each other, weltering in blood, and trodden down by their own comrades. The 43rd left twenty-two officers and three hundred men on the breach; two companies of the 52nd were blown to atoms by an explosion; and the 95th, as indeed every other regiment engaged, suffered in proportion.'

In the confusion of the attack the breach in the curtain had not been assaulted. This breach was the one that Wellington had ordered to be made earlier in the day and it had left the French with too little time in which to make it adequately protected against assault. It was considered to be the weakest of the three breaches, but was situated more to the rear of the other two and was guarded by a series of deep holes and cuts, and possibly because of this the troops seemed to ignore it and continued in vain to attack the breach of La Trinidad.

'Again did they attempt to pass this terrible gulf of steel and flame.' British troops hurl themselves against the breaches.

64

The West face of the Trinidad bastion today. This photograph was taken whilst standing in what was once the breach in the curtain.

The situation had become critical. The dead lay in ever-increasing heaps as men continued to fall; there was the stench of burning flesh; the wounded crawled around in the darkness struggling to free themselves and seeking shelter from the incessant streams of fire from the French defenders, and as yet the breach of the Santa Maria bastion had not yet been attacked.

Now, however, Captain Nicholas, of the Engineers, and Shaw, of the 43rd, collected about seventy men and decided to attack this breach. They passed over the deep cut at the foot of the breach and rushed up the ruins to the assault. Before they reached the top, however, the French poured out a concentrated fire of grape and musketry and the British were swept away from the slopes, Nicholas received a grape shot through his lungs from which he later died, whilst Shaw and the other survivors withdrew to seek shelter from the raking fire of the defences around them.

At length the desperate assaults began to fade as the frustrated and despairing British troops were continually driven from the breaches by the French, fighting like demons to keep them out. The British gathered in groups in the darkness and looked up despairingly at the breaches, whilst the French troops stepped from the ramparts, hurling fire-balls at their assailants by which they aimed their shots. It was said that at least forty separate assaults were made on the breaches, each of them repulsed, with almost 2,000 of Wellington's best men smashed against the defences. No impression had been made. The British began to ask themselves: 'what is to be done?'

66

Badajoz, 1812. From an old engraving.

Whilst the slaughter at the breaches had been in progress the attack upon the castle by Picton's 3rd Division had been raging with equal savagery. The division had moved forward shortly before ten o'clock with MacCarthy acting as guide. Colonel Williams, of the 60th, led three companies of his own regiment and the light companies of the division. These were followed by Kempt's three brigades, Campbell's brigade and two Portuguese regiments. The division moved forward in silence, but got off to an uneasy start. MacCarthy, leading the way, found himself leading the men across ground unknown to him and began to wonder whether he was taking the correct route. On several occasions he had to run ahead in order to ascertain that he was, in fact, on course. This in turn began to cause Picton some anxiety and he asked MacCarthy if he knew where he was leading the division. Suddenly the attack on the San Roque began.

MacCarthy:

'. . . the firing of the enemy's musketry, becoming brisk, increased the General's anxiety to be as contiguous as possible, previous to the general

67

assault, lest any occurrence should retard the operation of his division; and when I again advanced some distance to discover Major Burgoyne and returned, General Picton, emphatically expressing himself, said I was blind, he supposed, and going wrong; and drawing his sword, swore he would cut me down.'

Fortunately for MacCarthy, he managed to calm Picton down and they arrived at the first parallel, which they entered, and as they reached the end of it:

'the enemy's volcanic fire burst forth in every direction, long and far over the division and in every kind of combustible, as if all the stars, planets and meteors of the firmament, with innumerable moons emitting smaller ones in their course, were congregated together, and descending upon the heads of the besiegers.'

As the division moved forward to attack, Picton stumbled, wounded in the foot and was helped to the left of the column, command passing to General Kempt. The advance party, under Williams, moved to the Rivellas and crossed it by way of the dam or by wading through the water. The dam was so narrow, however, that it was only possible to cross it in single file and the French, aware of this, turned their guns on it. The dam was by now a seething mass of impatient, confused soldiers and each discharge from the French guns tore bloody lanes through them, whilst many of them slipped over the side and drowned in the inundation. Pressed from behind, the ladders parties could not move and the way across became blocked until MacCarthy, struggling forward, opened the way:

'I found the ladders left on the palisades in the fosse, and this barrier unbroken; in the exigence, I cried out, "Down with the paling!" and, aided by officers and men in rocking the fence, made the opening at which the divisions entered; and which being opposite the mound, then, "Up with the ladders!" – "What, up here?" said a brave officer, "Yes" was replied – and all seizing the ladders, pulled and pushed each other with them up the acclivity of the mound, as the shortest way to its summit.'

Joseph Donaldson, of the 94th:

'We still advanced, silent as before, saving the groaning of our wounded comrades, until we reached a sort of moat about fifty feet wide, formed by the inundation of the river; here we had to pass, rank entire, the passage being only capable of limiting one at a time. On this place the enemy had brought their guns to bear, and they kept up such a fire of grape and musketry on it, that it was a miracle any of us escaped. When we reached the other side we formed again, and advanced up the glacis, forcing our way through the palisades, and got into the ditch. The ladders by which we had to escalade the castle were not yet brought up, and the men were huddled

68

The colours of the Hesse-Darmstadt Regiment, captured by Private George Hatton of the 4th Foot.

on one another in such a manner that we could not move; we were now ordered to fix our bayonets. When we first entered the trench we thought ourselves comparatively safe, thinking we were out of range of their shot, but we were soon convinced of our mistake, for they opened several guns from angles which commanded the trench, and poured in grape shot upon us from every side, every shot of which took effect, and every volley of which was succeeded by the dying groans of those who fell.'

Private William Brown, of the 45th, wrote:

'. . . our Regiment, being on the right of the division, might be termed the Forlorn Hope, and suffered accordingly. The point at which we descended into the ditch was between two bastions, from both of which we experienced a dreadful fire of musketry, while from the body of the wall the enemy continued to pour, by means of boards placed on the parapet, whole showers of grenades, which they arranged in rows, and, being lighted with a match, the whole was upset, exploding amongst us in the ditch with horrid destruction. Coils of rope, in a friable state, strongly impregnated with tar, pitch and oil, were likewise employed by the enemy as a means of annoyance, which completely answered the purpose intended by scorching and scalding numbers in a dreadful manner.'

As each ladder was placed against the walls it was quickly mounted from top to bottom. The men at the head of the ladders were met by pikes, bayonets and musketry, and the French pushed their ladders from the walls. The deafening shouts, the crashing of falling ladders, and the loud shrieks of the crushed and wounded men added to the loud din of the fighting, and excited the soldiers waiting below who had, by now, reached a point of madness. They swarmed around the ladders and rushed to the tops, only to be tossed over by the waiting French who began to cry: 'Victory!'

William Brown again:

'Our men rushed up the ladders with the greatest impetuosity, but when near the top the whole broke down, and all that were on them were precipitated on the points of their comrades' bayonets, by which many received their death. We were then ordered to unfix our bayonets and sling our firelocks on our shoulders, which being done and a number of ladders brought, we immediately began to ascend. The ladder I chanced to be on was laid to the bottom of an embrasure, in which were a number of the enemy ready to receive us, and in front of them stood an officer with a pistol in each hand ready cocked. On the ladder a Grenadier officer of our regiment preceded us, who, when his head was nearly on a line with the enemy's feet, was fired at by the officer in front. Missing the contents of the pistol he instantly gave his opponent a back-slap across the legs with his sabre, who fell over into the ditch. Our officer then leapt into the embrasure, cutting down all that opposed him, and was immediately followed by the men. . .'

69

Looking down from the ramparts of the Castle. The 3rd Division placed its ladders at the foot of these walls to make its escalade.

The first ladders, in fact, had been placed in the wrong position. In their impetuosity the troops had rushed to the wall between the bastions of San Antonio and San Pedro, whereas Wellington had expressly ordered the escalade to take place at the actual wall of the castle, and now the British troops found themselves caught between the crossfire of the two bastions. The French poured a heavy fire into the red columns, as well as hurling down logs and large rocks and boulders. MacCarthy wrote:

'This place, and the whole face of the wall, being opposed by the guns of the citadel, were so swept by their discharges of round shot, broken shells, bundles of cartridges, and other missiles, and also from the top of the wall ignited shells, etc, that it was almost impossible to twinkle an eye on any man before he was knocked down.'

MacCarthy was placing the fallen ladders against the wall:

Illustrated on previous pages

The Storming of Badajoz, 1812. The attack on the Castle by Picton's 3rd Division. The bare-headed officer in the foreground is probably Lieutenant-Colonel Ridge, traditionally the first man into the town.

'and in returning to the longest ladder, planted against the wall on the right of the mound, it was my turn to fall – my right thigh was fractured by a ball which entered the upper part, and I fell upon a man who had just dropped at my side, with the calf of my leg and heel turned upwards. I instantly seized the trousers, and turned over the limb to preserve existence; and being in a spot most exposed to the guns, I requested a field-officer near to desire some of his men to carry me out of the streams of fire; but he turned himself

72

Another view of the Castle walls today.

away – and one of his men said, "I'll take you down, sir; can you stand!" – This good fellow took me on his back, but was obliged to drop me, and in a place more exposed.'

At length MacCarthy was moved to a more sheltered spot where he spent an uncomfortable night amongst the hundreds of other sufferers until he was moved late in the afternoon of the next day.

Joseph Donaldson, of the 94th:

'Our situation at this time was truly appalling. The attack had commenced at the breaches towards our left, and the cannon and musketry which played upon our troops from every quarter of the town attacked, kept up a continual roll of thunder, and their incessant flash one quivering sheet of lightening; to add to the awfulness of the scene, a mine was sprung at the breach, which carried up, in its dreadful blaze, the mangled limbs and bodies of many of our comrades.
'When the ladders were placed, each eager to mount, crowded them in such a way that many of them broke, and the poor fellows who had nearly reached the top, were precipitated a height of thirty or forty feet, and were impaled on the bayonets of their comrades below; other ladders were pushed aside by the enemy on the walls, and fell with a crash on those in the ditch; while more who got to the top without accident were shot on reaching the parapet, and tumbling headlong, brought down those beneath them.'

73

An hour had passed and still no impression had been made on the castle. General Kempt had been wounded and command passed back into the hands of Picton, who had recovered from his earlier wound and had reached the foot of the castle walls just after the failure of the first attack. A second attack was to be made and once again the ranks of British troops swarmed around the ladders and with incredible courage ascended amidst the shower of projectiles which the French hurled down on them only to be denied again, to hear the French cries of 'Victory!' as one by one the ladders were overturned and pushed from the walls plunging the assailants headlong into the baffled and confused crowds below.

At this point, however, Colonel Ridge, of the 5th, seized one of the ladders and placed it against the castle where the wall was lower, and where an embrasure afforded some protection. He called out loudly for his men to follow him and was quickly followed by a Grenadier officer of the 5th, Canch, who placed a second ladder at the wall. Ridge ascended the ladder so quickly that before the French could push it away, the weight had become too great and the ladder placed firmly against the wall. Ridge pressed on amidst the pikes and bayonets with his sword guarding his head and with the bayonets of those behind him thrust upwards to protect him. Then, miraculously, both Ridge and Canch and a few others were standing on the ramparts.

'A general rush to the ladders now took place,' wrote Grattan, 'and the dead and wounded, that lay in the ditch were indiscriminately trampled upon, for humanity was nowhere to be found. A frightful butchery followed this success; and the shouts of our soldiery mingled with the cries of the Frenchmen, supplicating for mercy, or in the agonies of death, were heard at a great distance.'

The British troops rushed furiously up the ladders and for the first time the tide turned in their favour. They had paid dearly for this success, however, with the blood of many of their comrades, and now the French defenders paid their price for the defence they had put up and for the damage they had inflicted upon their assailants. The British had become infuriated by their continual failure and little mercy was shown:

'Few, very few of those who had assisted in raising the pile of dead that now nearly filled the ditch, were left to boast of their deeds.'

One of the first up the ladders was Lieutenant Macpherson, of the 45th, closely followed by Sir Edward Packenham. As he reached the top he found that the ladder was about three feet too short. Unperturbed, he called out loudly above the noise to those below to raise it more vertically and, as he pushed with great strength from the

Opposite:
The 5th Division escalade the ramparts of the San Vincente bastion. Note the spikes and the barrels of gunpowder thrown down from the ramparts. Also, note the way the British troops stand on each other's shoulders, the ladders being too short.

The Storming of Badajoz.
This spirited painting gives a
good impression of the
height of the town's walls.
The debris from the
breached wall has
conveniently formed a
causeway for the British
troops to climb.

Storming of Badajoz by the 83rd Regiment, 1812. A drawing showing some of the savage hand-to-hand fighting that raged during the storming. Note the expressions on the faces of two men struggling in the foreground.

wall at the top, the men below, with a loud cheer, brought it nearer at the base. This was done so suddenly, however, that Macpherson found himself level with the rampart and before he could defend himself a French soldier had levelled his musket against his body and fired. Luckily the bullet struck one of the Spanish silver buttons on his waistcoat, causing it to change direction and glance off. Macpherson was left with two fractured ribs, one of which pressed against his lungs and made breathing difficult. He did not fall, however, but clung to the top of the ladder, unable to advance and unaware of the extent of his wound. Packenham climbed past him but he too was severely wounded. Suddenly the ladder broke and death seemed certain as a chevaux-de-frise waited below. But somehow Macpherson managed, by getting to the back of the ladder, to descend to the ditch in safety, where he lay unconcious for some time.

More and more British troops dashed up the ladders to consolidate their position. The left brigade, the 5th, 77th, 83rd and 94th, under Colonel Campbell, moved along to that part of the castle wall that had been breached during a previous siege and not properly prepared. The ladders were placed and the men scrambled up. Lieutenant Parr Kingsmill, of the 88th:

'The ladders being at length placed, the troops with three cheers courageously ascended and nothing was soon heard but mingled cries of despair and shouts of victory. Several ladders, having too great a weight upon them, broke down, and the men were precipitated on the bayonets of their comrades below; they continued to push up in crowds, determined to reach the ramparts or die in the attempt. The ladder I mounted, like many others, was unfortunately too short, and I found that no exertion I could make would enable me to gain the embrasure or to descend. In this unhappy state, expecting immediate death from the hands of the furious looking Frenchmen in the embrasure, I heard a voice above call out, "Mr Kingsmill, is that you?" I answered "Yes," and the same voice cried out "Oh murther! murther! what will we do to get you up at all with that scrawdeen of a ladtherr? But here goes! Hold my leg Bill," and by throwing himself flat on his face in the embrasure he extended his brawny arm down the wall, and seizing me by the collar, with herculean force, landed me, as he said himself, "cleaver and clave" on the ramparts.'

Kingsmill found himself standing on the ramparts amongst several French soldiers, crowding round the gun in the embrasure. One of them still held the lighted match in his hand by which the blue flame lit up his fearsome, bronzed face which Kingsmill remembered long afterwards; a Grenadier leant against the gun, bleeding profusely from a wound in the head, others just sat around in despair and 'their huge bushy moustaches and mouths blackened with biting the cartridges, presented to the eye of a young soldier at least an appearance sufficiently formidable'.

Meanwhile Ridge formed his men at the ramparts and called to them, 'come on my lads! let's be the first to seize the governor,' and he led his men over the surprised and amazed garrison, over the works and through the darkness into the castle. The French retired and formed in an open space by the castle gate. For a short time the firing stopped and Ridge and his men groped their way through the darkness, following the ramparts until they came to a passage leading to the centre of the castle. As they advanced a column was seen and the men stopped. Ridge called out, 'Why do you hesitate? Forward!' and with caution they continued to advance. They had gone a little further when the French were seen again and immediately the British troops opened fire upon them. The French returned the fire and the gallant Ridge fell, hit by a musket ball in the breast and he died almost at once. The French were scattered, however, and after leaving a few men to guard their commander's body the British troops pressed on.

They advanced through the gloom of the castle firing as they went with the French falling back before them. When they reached the castle gate, which led out into the town, the British found the French had closed it as they had retreated. The inner gate was forced quite easily but the outer gate was secured much stronger. A small wicket gate was left open, however, but the French opened up a heavy fire on anyone who attempted to pass it. Colonel Campbell therefore ordered his men to retire to within the inner gate of the castle and directed the 5th to form up, face the gate, and wait there. Soon afterwards they heard the sound of approaching soldiers.

Governor Phillipon, General Veiland and other French staff officers were assembled in the Place de Saint Jean, when suddenly a Spanish officer arrived to report that the British had penetrated the castle. Phillipon and his staff were stunned by this report and could hardly believe it. They had placed their baggage and supplies inside and in the event of the town falling they had hoped to make the castle the last place of defence. The sound of battle could be heard in that direction, however, and so Phillipon decided to find out for himself, and with several other officers he rushed to the castle but found nobody but the French troops defending it. It seemed that the Spanish officer had panicked when some shells rolled over the ramparts and exploded. A few moments later Lieutenant Lavigne, of the Dragoons, galloped over seeking the governor. He, too, had come from the castle and reported that the British were escalading the walls. The fallacy of the first report caused this second report to be doubted; it would be a disaster for the French and seemed impossible. Nevertheless, Phillipon decided to send some troops over to reinforce the position but precious time was lost in hesitation.

The Hessian Colonel, upon whom rested the defence of the castle, had with him a number of his own regiment and a few French soldiers and a small detachment of artillery. On hearing this latest report, however, Phillipon sent four companies of the 88th Regiment to assist in the defence of the castle but they arrived too late and were thrown back by a heavy firing from the British troops inside. At the same time two companies of the 9th Light Infantry were marching towards the castle but had become lost and were soon entangled in the confusion at the breaches, and there they remained throughout the rest of the fighting. The loss of the castle came as a great shock to the French and now Phillipon knew there could be no retreat as the place in which he had hoped to make a final stand had now fallen. When the news of the loss spread to the French troops fighting elsewhere, panic and disorder began to set in.

By now hundreds of enraged, victorious British troops had gained the castle walls, whilst at the foot of the walls Lieutenant Macpherson had regained his senses and tried to raise himself. His broken ribs made it difficult for him to breathe but in his attempt to rise, the bone which was pressing against his lung was forced from its place, the pain was eased and his breathing made comfortable again.

80

He rose and climbed a ladder to the top of the ramparts, which were now gained, this object being to capture the French flag which flew in the tower of the castle. The French continued to defend every post but their resistance was now subsiding, and the infuriated British soldiers set about bayonetting the defenders without mercy.

'I at length found my way to the tower,' he wrote afterwards, 'where I perceived the sentry still at his post. With my sword drawn, I seized him, and desired him in French to show me the way to the colours. He replied "Je ne sais pas". I, upon this, gave him a slight cut across the face, saying at the same time, "Vous le savez present," at which he dashed his arms to the ground, and, striking his breast, said, as he raised his head and pointed to his heart, "Frappez, je suis Francais!" his manner at the same time indicating that the colour was there. I could not wait to provide for the safety of this brave fellow; so I called out loudly for a non-commissioned officer to take charge of him, so that he should not be hurt. One step forward, when, giving him instructions to protect the gallant soldier, I ascended the tower; but my precaution was vain, for I afterwards discovered that this noble fellow was amongst the dead.'

On reaching the top of the tower Macpherson found the French colour still flying. He tore it down and for want of something better he took off his jacket and hoisted it on the staff as a substitute for the British flag.

The British troops inside the castle had now secured the gate and they waited for reinforcements to arrive. The troops swarmed over the rocks at the foot of the walls and more ladders were placed against the ramparts and were quickly filled from top to bottom by the eager and furious troops who had begun to sense victory. The few French troops who were found inside the castle were quickly put to sword, amongst whom were Chief of Battalion Schmalkalder and Adjutant-Major Schulz, of the Hessians, and a Captain of artillery, D'André Saint-Victor.

Whilst the fighting at the breaches and the castle had been going on Wellington had been watching intently from a hillock not far from the main breach. With him were the Prince of Orange and Lord March. By one-thirty in the morning it had become clear to him that the place could not be taken by storm. 1,800 of his best men were dead or wounded and lay struggling to free themselves in a space of not more than a hundred yards square. Surgeon James McGrigor and a Doctor Forbes joined Wellington at his vantage point. McGrigor wrote:

'Soon after our arrival, an officer came up with an unfavourable report of the assault, announcing that Colonel Macleod and several officers were killed, with heaps of men, who choked the approach to the breach. At the place where we stood, we were within hearing of the voices of the assailants

The Forlorn Hope at
Badajoz. An extremely
romantic version of the
assault on Badajoz. The
cavalry took no part at all in
the siege, despite the two
Life Guards in the painting,
also the storming took place
in complete darkness, not as
shown here.

and of the assailed; and it was now painful to notice that the voices of our
countrymen had become fainter, while the French cry of "avancez, etrillons
ces anglais," became stronger. Another officer came up with a still more
unfavourable report, that no progress was being made; for almost all the
officers were killed, and no more left to lead on the men, of whom a great
number had fallen. At this moment I cast my eyes on the countenance of
Lord Wellington, lit up by the glare of the torch held by Lord March; I shall
never forget it to the last moment of my existence, and I could even now
sketch it. The jaw had fallen, and the face was of unusual length, while the
torchlight gave his countenance a lurid aspect; but still the expression of the
face was firm.'

This report was just one of a succession informing Wellington of the
failure of his men to storm the town. His best men had been smashed
on the defences and finally he ordered the bugler to sound the recall.
Suddenly an officer came riding out of the gloom crying 'Where is
Lord Wellington?' It was Picton's aide-de-camp. 'Who's that?'
asked Wellington, and the officer replied 'Lieutenant Tyler'. 'Ah,
Tyler, – well?' asked Wellington again. 'General Picton has taken
the castle, my Lord,' was Tyler's reply, to which Wellington
exclaimed: 'Then the place is ours!'

Tyler was immediately sent back to Picton with orders that he
must keep possession of the castle at all costs. Picton's men needed
no such order, however, for they had already secured the castle gates
and parties of them had begun to move along the ramparts towards
the breaches. But the French had heavily barricaded the gates

82

communicating with the ramparts when they had retreated from the castle and these iron bound barriers proved to be difficult to open by the means which the British troops had at their disposal, and also reinforcements from the San Vincente bastion had arrived and an attempt to retake the castle was made. The French tried to retake it by an old gate, leading towards the town, which soon became filled with holes as the French poured out a stream of musketry. In return, the British troops inside the castle turned a gun on the gate and fired it twice making two large holes. An old handspike was placed under its breech to depress it and the gate remained securely in British hands. The French efforts to retake the castle failed as more and more British troops climbed the walls and entered.

The confidence of the garrison was severely shaken as the castle was secured and unless it was retaken any attempt to drive the British away from the breaches would eventually prove useless. The reinforcements that had arrived in the last attempt to recapture the castle, but had failed, had previously been engaged in defending the San Vincente bastion. The struggle had been in progress since the general assault on the town began around ten o'clock.

The storming parties consisted of the light companies of the 4th, 30th, 38th and 44th Regiments under the command of Lieutenant-Colonel Brooke, of the 4th Kings Own. These were supported by the battalion companies of the 4th, whilst the 30th and 44th remained in reserve under General Walker. They advanced silently up the glacis and could soon hear the voices of the French sentries in the guard house. Suddenly, one of them challenged the column and a hail of bullets followed from other sentries on duty. The guiding engineer fell dead and in the confusion the Portuguese troops dropped their ladders and fled into the night. The ladders were picked up by the light company men who pushed on to the assault. First they beat down the palisade over the covered way and then descended the twelve feet from the top of the counterscarp into the ditch. The cunette in the ditch was itself six feet deep and five feet wide but it was jumped, and then they set about scaling the walls of the scarp which were twenty feet high with an incline of twelve feet above that. The ladders were then placed against the right flank of the bastion.

As the troops began to crowd around the bottom of the ladders a mine was exploded beneath them and a shower of live shells and logs of wood was hurled down from the ramparts into their midst. The guns in the tower a hundred yards away opened up with grape shot and scores of men dropped from the ladders. Some of the survivors said afterwards that half of the light company men were killed almost at once. Brooke saw it was hopeless and changed the plan of attack. In order to keep down the fire of the defenders two companies of the 44th were extended along the edge of the ditch and opened fire on

the defenders that flanked the left face of the San Vincente, whilst Brooke attacked a weaker spot on the left face close to the salient. The men here quickly raised three ladders close together to enable the men to support each other and they were quickly mounted, only for the men to find they were about seven feet too short. Fortunately, an embrasure was found and one of the men was hoisted up to the sill and in turn pulled up his comrades. The French tried furiously to dislodge them but could not get to grips with them, neither with pike nor bayonet. The leading British troops were falling fast but as more and more of them gained the ramparts the French defenders were overrun and the bastion cleared.

Major Piper, of the 4th, leading his men forward in support, was stepping into the bastion when he received a wound from a musket ball, which knocked him over onto the piles of dead and wounded. This probably saved his life as a moment later the magazine in the bastion exploded, killing many British and French troops alike. As soon as General Walker had reached the top of the ramparts he formed up his brigade. One half of the 4th, under the command of Major Piper, was sent to clear out some French troops who had begun firing at them from a large house at the rear of the bastion. The rest of the brigade under Walker himself formed and began advancing towards the breaches whilst Leith sent in the 38th and the 15th Portuguese to secure the bastion. Walker's men began to clear the French from their positions but their advance came to a halt between bastions 4 and 5. Here the 28th Light Infantry and the 58th of the line had been putting up a stiff resistance and had checked the British troops. Walker, sword in hand, led his men forward to attack but as he dashed forward to clear a traverse a field gun was fired and he fell to the ground, seriously wounded. As the men rushed to aid their fallen General a lighted match was seen burning along the ground and a cry went up: 'a mine! a mine!' The lighted match, however, was in fact just the flame of a portfire thrown by a gunner which had flared up. But the British troops were in the grip of their imaginations and the cry caused a panic and they staggered back in disorder. General Veiland chose this moment to bring forward some French reserves, commanded by Captain Malheste and charging forward they drove the British back through the streets to the ramparts, pitching them over at bayonet point and eventually driving them right back to the San Vincente. Here, however, Leith had posted his reserve, the 38th, under Colonel Nugent, and as the French drew nearer they waited and then delivered a devastating volley which scattered the French counter-attack and ended the panic amongst their own comrades. The bugles sounded the advance and again they began to make their way forward to the breaches.

The detachment of the 4th Kings Own under Major Piper was

85

passing through the town in an attempt to attack the defenders of the breaches in rear. Captain Edward Hopkins was one of the detachment.

'The enemy retired from the buildings on our approach and Major Piper did not return to the ramparts, but moved into the body of the town. Could we have divested our minds of the real situation of the town it might have been imagined that the inhabitants were preparing for some grand fete, as all the houses in the streets and squares were brilliantly illuminated from the top of the first floor, with numerous lamps. This illumination was truly remarkable, not a living creature to be seen, but a continual low buzz and whisper around us, and we now and then perceived a small lattice gently open and re-shut, as if more closely to observe the scene of a small English party perambulating the town in good order, the bugler now at the head blowing his instrument. Some of our men and officers now fell wounded; at first we did not know where the shots came from, but soon observed they were from the sills of the doors.'

Piper's party were unable to reach the breaches but succeeded in gaining the Place de Saint Jean, where Phillipon had earlier made his headquarters. Hopkins again:

'We soon arrived at a large church facing some grand houses, in a sort of square. The party here drew up, and it was at first proposed to take possession of the church, but that idea was abandoned. We made several prisoners leading mules laden with loose ball cartridges in large wicker baskets, which they stated they were conveying from the magazine to the breaches. After securing the prisoners, ammunition, etc, we moved from the square with the intention of forcing our way upon the ramparts. We went up a small street towards them but met with such opposition as obliged us to retire with loss. We again found ourselves in the square.'

There had also been a fierce struggle on the other side of the town near the river by the gate of Las Palmas. Phillipon had heard that the San Vincente had been attacked and had seen the failure of the attempt to retake the castle. As a last desperate attempt to drive the British from the town, he ordered the forty or so mounted dragoons and chasseurs with him to charge the Place de Las Palmas. This, too, proved futile and nearly all the horses were either killed or wounded and the riders driven off by the volleys of British musketry. It was now impossible to stop the British. Phillipon himself was cut off from his men but along with General Veiland and about fifty men and with a few cavalry he managed, with some difficulty, to make his escape across the bridge to the fort San Christobal.

During his last attempt to check the British Phillipon had sent one of his staff, Captain De Grasse, to try and contact the body of French troops at the breaches. The governor understood that a large body of his troops still kept its formation and he hoped that most of them

Illustrated on previous pages
The Siege of Badajoz, 1812.
The fighting inside the town.

88

The Gate of Las Palmas, Badajoz. Phillipon and the rest of the French survivors escaped through this gate and crossed the old Roman bridge [behind the camera].

might be able to fight their way back to him at the gate of Las Palmas, but De Grasse found the streets blocked by the men from Walker's brigade and the French themselves surrendering fast as the resistance crumbled. Leith's entire division was now marching towards the breaches with its bugles sounding in advance, and when they were answered by those of Picton's division all French opposition collapsed.

Lamare:

'. . . doubt and dismay took possession of their minds, they fled about the street and fled in disorder. Cries of "Victory!" and frightful groans were heard; confusion was at its height.'

The gallant French troops who had defended the breaches had remained steady throughout all the assaults until now. Without leadership and without orders they dispersed. Some small groups retired into various houses in the town where they continued to defend themselves until dawn, but for the most part the exhausted French troops, many of them wounded, felt further resistance was pointless and they broke their arms and surrendered.

It was now two o'clock in the morning of 7 April. Wellington had

Badajoz taken by Storm on 6 April 1812 by the Allied Army under Lord Wellington.

just received news of the success of Leith's assault and he ordered the 4th and light divisions to reform and advance to the breaches again. This time they met with no opposition and at last entered the town.

'I was lying upon the grass,' wrote George Simmons, 'having the most gloomy thoughts of the termination of this sad affair, when a staff officer

rode up and said, "Lord Wellington orders the Light Division to return immediately and attack the breaches." We moved back to this bloody work as if nothing had happened. Never were braver men congregated together for such a purpose. We entered the ditches, and passed over the bodies of our brave fellows who had fallen and dashed forward to the breaches. Only a few random shots were fired, and we entered without opposition. Firing was now going on in several parts of the town, and we were not long in

The Santa Maria bastion as it looks today. The walls were breached at the point behind the trees and bushes to the right, none of which were there in 1812. The foreground was once the ditch which was full of the dead and dying of the 4th and Light Divisions.

chiming in with the rest of them. The prisoners were secured and the place was given up to be plundered and pillaged.'

Edward Costello was still coming to his senses and was unaware that the town had fallen:

'After the horrible and well-known scene of carnage had lasted for some time, the fire gradually slackened from within the breach, and I heard a cheering which I knew to proceed from within the town, and shortly afterwards a cry of "Blood and 'ounds! Where's the light division? – the town's our own – hurrah!" This proceeded, no doubt, from some of the third division. I now attempted to rise, but, from a wound which I had received, but at what time I know not, found myself unable to stand. A musket ball had passed through the lower part of my right leg – two others had perforated my cap. At the moment of this discovery I saw two or three men moving towards me, who I was glad to find belonged to the Rifles. One of them, named O'Brien, of the same company as myself, immediately exclaimed "What! is that you, Ned? – we thought all you ladder men done for." He then assisted me to rise.'

Although moving only with great difficulty Costello reached the top of the breach. After climbing the chevaux-de-frise he crossed a plank of wood over a trench and was inside the walls and started into the town. He soon felt drops of blood trickling down his face and discovered that one of the balls, in passing through his cap, had torn the skin of his head.

Some sporadic fighting still continued, however. Shortly after the last attack at the breaches Grattan was involved in placing some casks of gunpowder beneath the dam at the San Roque, when suddenly:

'I was struck by a musket-ball in the left breast; I staggered back, but did not fall, and Thompson bandaging my breast and shoulder with his handkerchief, caused me to be removed inside the ravelin.'

Eventually, exhausted through loss of blood, Grattan was supported back to the trenches. Kincaid heard the castle had fallen shortly after his men had reformed for another attack. The breaches had been abandoned and they were ordered forward to take possession of them.

'On our arrival, we found them entirely evacuated, and had not occasion to fire another shot; but we found the utmost difficulty, and even danger, in getting in in the dark, even without opposition. As soon as we succeeded in establishing our battalion inside, we sent piquets into the different streets and lanes leading from the breach, and kept the remainder in hand until day should throw some light on our situation. When I was in the act of posting the piquets, a man of ours brought me a prisoner, telling me that he was the governor; but immediately the other said that he had only called himself so, the better to ensure his protection; and then added that he was the colonel of one of the French regiments, and that all his surviving officers were assembled at his quarters in a street close by, and would surrender themselves to any officer who would go with him for that purpose.'

Kincaid took two or three men with him and duly took the French officers prisoner. They could not understand how the town had fallen, and even Kincaid thought himself lucky to be 'lording it over the officers of a French battalion'. The prisoners were marched back to the breach, amongst them a big Dutchman, 'with medals enough on his left breast, to furnish a tolerable toy shop'. As they made their way back other French soldiers were lurking about, waiting to surrender themselves; so many in fact that Kincaid's column was almost fired upon by a British piquet thinking they were a body of rallied Frenchmen.

Costello had entered the town using his rifle as a crutch. With him were a few other riflemen and they could hear the firing and cheering going on in the other parts of the town, and thought the fighting was still continuing. As they turned a corner they noticed some men and from the light that shone from a window opposite

they could tell they were French. They quickly dispersed but one man rushed forward with his musket.

Costello:

'O'Brien sprang forward and wrestled the firelock from his grasp. A feeling of revenge, prompted by the suffering I endured from my wounds, actuated my feelings, and I exclaimed "O'Brien, let me have the pleasure of shooting this rascal, for he may be the man who has brought me to the state I am now in!" I then presented my musket close to his breast, with the full intention of shooting him through the body, but as my finger was about to press the trigger, he fell upon his knees and implored mercy.'

Costello let the Frenchman live, however, and they began to look round for a house where they could find some refreshments. The first house they reached was locked and they were forced to shoot the lock off the door. Inside they found a Spanish woman crying and praying for mercy. She produced some spirits and some chocolate which Costello enjoyed and then they left in search of something better. They headed for the market place.

'It was a dark night, and the confusion and uproar that prevailed in the town may be better imagined than described. The shouts and oaths of drunken soldiers in quest of more liquor, the reports of fire-arms and crashing in of doors, together with the appalling shrieks of hapless women, might have induced anyone to have believed himself in the regions of the damned.'

The sacking of Badajoz had begun.

Illustrated on previous pages
The Storming of Badajoz. Lithograph after R. Caton-Woodville. Wellington is cheered by his men as he surveys the carnage in the breaches.

5

Aftermath

'Badajoz, one of the richest and most beautiful towns in the south of Spain, whose inhabitants had witnessed its siege in silent terror for one and twenty days, and who had been shocked by the frightful massacre that had just taken place at its walls, was now about to be plunged into all the horrors that are, unfortunately, unavoidable upon an enterprise such as a town taken by storm.'

William Grattan wrote these words as he began to describe the shocking events that followed the fall of Badajoz. The victorious British soldiers, driven to the point of madness by the fury and violence of the assaults, embarked upon an orgy of rape, drunkenness and pillage. They had endured and suffered during the last twenty-one days a siege of miserable proportions in often terrible conditions. But despite this they had got on with their work and kept themselves busy in the trenches. Now the town had fallen however, and their anger found vent as Oman wrote:

'in misconduct far surpassing that which would have followed a pitched battle where the losses had been equally great.'

The Spanish people had never shown much hospitality towards the British soldiers and now the army in Badajoz 'dissolved into a dangerous mob of intoxicated soldiers'.

'In the first burst,' wrote Grattan, 'all the wine and spirit stores were ransacked from top to bottom: and it required just a short time for the men to get into that fearful state that was alike dangerous to all officers and soldiers, or the inhabitants of the city. Casks of the choicest wines and brandy were dragged into the streets, and when the men had drunk as much as they fancied, the heads of the vessels were stove in, or the casks otherwise so broken that the liquor ran about in streams.'

Inside the town many animals had been gathered including sheep, horses, and oxen that had belonged to the garrison. These were quickly taken and herded back to the camp. Inside the castle more animals had been gathered, as Phillipon had hoped that in the event of the town falling he might still be able to hold out there for a few days more. Unfortunately for Phillipon the castle had fallen and all hell was let loose.

LIEUT COLONEL. RIDGE 2 BATT
of the 5.ᵗʰ Regt of Foot
WHO WAS KILLED AT THE SIEGE of BADAJOS
THIS PORTRAIT IS A TESTIMONY
OF THE LOVE AND RESPECT
in which he was held by his
BROTHER OFFICERS.

Lieutenant-Colonel Ridge of the 5th Regiment of Foot. The first man to enter the town but killed soon afterwards.

'The scenes in the castle that night,' wrote Blakeney, 'were of a most deplorable and terrific nature: murders, robberies and every species of debauchery and obscenity were seen, notwithstanding the exertions of the officers to prevent them . . . The howling of the dogs, the crowing of cocks, the penetrating cackle of thousands of geese, the mournful bleating of sheep, the furious bellowing of wounded oxen maddened by being continually goaded and shot at ferociously charging through the streets, were mixed with accompaniments loudly trumpeted forth by mules and donkeys and always by the deep and bellow baying of the large Spanish half-wolves, half-bloodhounds which guarded the whole. Add to this the shrill screaming of affrighted children, the piercing shrieks of frantic women, the groans of the wounded, the savage and discordant yells of drunkards firing at everything and in all directions and the continued roll of musketry kept up in error on the shattered gateway; and you may imagine an uproar such as one would think could only issue from the regions of Pluto; and this din was maintained throughout the night.'

98

The Surrender of the French
Garrison. Despite the two
pictured here the French
had no eagles with them in
Badajoz.

Private William Brown of the 45th Regiment, wrote:

'When the garrison surrendered, leave for two hours was given to us to go to
the town, camp or wherever we pleased, but the town was universally
preferred. All rushed to the gate which communicated with it, which
caused a great deal of noise and squabbling, for the enemy had built up the
gateway as a means of defence, leaving a narrow passage through which but
one man could pass at a time. They all, however, got to the town soon
enough for the poor inhabitants, who were by many of our men shamefully
and barbarously treated. There was not, I believe, a house in the whole
town that was not ransacked from top to bottom – murder, rape, and robbery
were committed with the greatest impunity. The first building I entered

99

was a church, which the French had occupied as a provision store, and was at the time well filled with bags of flour, bread, biscuit and leaf tobacco. On one side were casks of liquor to the very roof. Each soldier, as he entered seized one for himself, and, having set it on one end, staved in the other with the butt of his firelock, then knelt down and drank what he pleased, which, in many cases, was not a little. In a short time, numbers got intoxicated, when all became confusion and uproar. The casks were upset, and the liquor poured on the floor until the church was nearly knee-deep, into which some in their folly threw themselves, that they might have it to say they had swum in rum, brandy and wine.

'During the day I entered many genteel houses, all full of our men who were busy pillaging: and what could not be carried away they in mere wantonness, destroyed. But all this was harmless, and might be termed as nothing when contrasted with some of the atrocities perpetrated in this devoted town . . . Determined to leave such a scene of riot and outrage, I proceeded along the street in which were exhibited every crime that could render man contemptible and disgrace human nature. At last arriving at the ground of the preceding night's encounter, a very different scene presented itself from that which I had just left. There lust and rapine were perpetrating every crime and at the moment trampling upon every principle sacred and civil, moral and religious; at that very instant were the demons of rage ruining everything good and virtuous, destroying the properties and violating the rights of every family and of every habitation. But here reigned a still and solemn silence; not a sound was heard, not a voice arose to disturb the awful pause, save the faint groans of the wounded and dying . . . Amongst the slain I saw many of my comrades and associates, with whom I had travelled many a long and weary mile. Some with whom I was intimately acquainted, and with whom but yesterday I had conversed freely, now lay stretched in their gore.'

The accounts left to us by the men who witnessed the storming and the terrible aftermath read like horror stories, even by today's standards, and they are sometimes hard to believe and certainly impossible to add to. Therefore I think it best if the men of Badajoz tell their own story. William Lawrence:

'Our troops found the city illuminated to welcome them, but nevertheless then began all the horrors that generally attended a capture by assault – plunder, waste, destruction of property, drunkenness and debauchery. I was myself exempt from all this owing to my wounds, which kept me in camp at the time the town was taken; but though I was at least a mile off, I could distinctly hear the clamour of the rabble as the guns and musketry had ceased; and next morning I hobbled as best I could into the town with the help of the handle of a sergeant's pike chopped up as to form a stick, and there sure enough I found a pretty state of affairs. Pipes of wine had been rolled into the streets and tapped by driving the heads in, for anyone to drink of them who liked, and when the officers tried to keep order by throwing all of these over that they could, the men that were in a state of drunkenness lay down to drink out of the gutters, which were thus running with all sorts of liquors; doors were blown open all through the city, both

100

upstairs and down, by placing charges at the keyhole and so removing the locks. I myself saw that morning a naked priest launched into the streets and flogged down it by some of our men who had a grudge against him for the treatment they had met at a convent, when staying in the town before.'

Charles Von Hodenberg was an officer of the King's German Legion and he, too, was appalled by what he saw in Badajoz:

'In less than an hour after it fell into our possession it looked as if centuries had gradually completed its devastation. The surviving soldier, after storming a town, considers it as his indisputable property, and thinks himself at liberty to commit any enormity by way of indemnifying himself for the risking of his life. The bloody strife has made him insensible to every better feeling; his lips are parched by the extraordinary exertions that he has made, and from necessity, as well as inclination, his first search is for liquor. This once obtained, every trace of human nature vanishes, and no brutal outrage can be named which he does not commit. The town was not only plundered of every article which the soldiers could carry off, but whatever was useless to them or could not be removed was wantonly destroyed. Wherever an officer appeared in the streets the wretched inhabitants flocked around him with terror and despair, embraced his knees, and supplicated his protection. But it was vain to oppose the soldiers: there were 10,000 of them crowding the streets, the greater part drunk, discharging their pieces in all directions – it was difficult to escape them unhurt.

'A couple of hundred of their women from the camp poured also into the place, when it was barely taken, to have their share of the plunder. They were, if possible, worse than the men. Gracious God! such tigresses in the shape of women! I sickened when I saw them coolly step over the dying, indifferent to their cries for a drop of water, and deliberately search the pockets of the dead for money, or even divest them of their bloody coats. But no more of these scenes of horror. I went deliberately into the town to harden myself to the sight of human misery – but I have had enough of it: my blood has been frozen with the outrages I have witnessed.'

Surgeon James McGrigor had gone into the town in order to find out the number of wounded:

'In a little time the whole of the soldiers appeared to be in a state of mad drunkenness. In every street, and in every corner we met them forcing their way like furies into houses, firing through the keyholes of the doors so as to force locks, or at any person they saw at a window imploring mercy. In passing some houses which they had entered we heard the shrieks of females, and sometimes the groans of whom they were no doubt butchering. All was disorder and dire confusion. Three soldiers whom we met in the streets, having lost all respect for the uniform of an officer, looked at him with a threatening aspect if addressed; and if threatened, they would sometimes point their muskets at him.'

John Cooke, of the 43rd, wrote afterwards:

'The place was eventually completely sacked by our troops: every atom of furniture broken: beds ripped open in search of treasures; and the street

101

literally strewed with articles knee deep. A convent was in flames, and the poor nuns in dishabille, striving in vain to burrow themselves into some place of security; however, that was impossible; the town was alive, and every house filled with mad soldiers from the cellar to the once solitary garret.'

George Simmons, of the 95th, managed to find something to eat:

'I went into a genteel house. The Spaniard told me the French Quartermaster-General had lived with him. He showed me the officer's room. I found a bottle of wine and two glasses upon the table. There was a piece of paper upon which he had made a rough sketch of the two breaches, and had represented the way our columns would move to the attack. He also had marked where the ladders would be placed to avoid some water in the ditch, and which was the only place where their shot could have effect. I suppose the water had been turned into the ditch for this purpose. The Spaniard said the two officers went out in great alarm. I sat down and drank the bottle of wine and got some eggs and bacon fried.'

One officer had gone into the town in the hope of affording protection to a family with whom he had stayed after the battle of Talavera, but the house had been plundered, the furniture destroyed and the family gone:

'The town had now become a scene of plunder and devastation; our soldiers and our women, in a state of intoxication had lost all control over themselves. These, together with numbers of Spanish and Portuguese, who had come into the city from the neighbourhood in search of plunder, filled every street. Many were dispossessed of their booty by others; and these interchanges of plunder in many cases were not effected without bloodshed, when the party about to be deprived of his spoils was sufficiently sober to offer resistance. Our soldiers had taken possession of the shops, stationed themselves behind counters, and were selling the goods contained in them. These were again displaced by more numerous parties, who became shopkeepers in their turn; and thus, one set replaced another until order was restored.'

This officer was glad to leave this scene of 'infuriated licentiousness' but returned to the town on 9 April:

'The scene which presented itself on my arrival would require the pen of a Hogarth to describe. Hundreds of both sexes were lying in the streets in a state of helpless intoxication, habited in various costume. Amongst them were those who had fallen by the hands of their own comrades. Nor was it easy to discriminate between the drunken and the dead; both were often equally pale and motionless. Churches and convents, shops and stores with wines and spirituous liquors, private houses and palaces, had all been plundered. The actors of these excesses were attired in the habits of priests with broad-brimmed hats of monks and of nuns, and in the dresses of grandees and of ladies of rank.'

102

Edward Costello and his companions had reached the market place. Numbers of Spanish prisoners were rushing out from a jail, still bearing their chains, and men from the 5th and 88th Regiments were walking around holding lighted candles. They went down a street opposite and entered a house occupied by men from the 3rd Division:

'I had not long been seated at the fire,' wrote Costello, 'which was blazing up the chimney, fed by mahogany chairs, broken up for the purpose, when I heard screams for mercy from an adjoining room. On hobbling in, I found an old man, the proprietor of the house, on his knees imploring mercy of a soldier who had levelled his musket at him. I with difficulty prevented the man from shooting him, as he complained that the Spaniard would not give up his money. I immediately informed the wretched landlord in Spanish, as well as I was able, that he could only save his life by surrendering his cash. Upon this he brought out with trembling hands a large bag of dollars from under the mattress of the bed.'

The bag contained about 150 dollars which he promptly shared amongst the soldiers, Costello's share being about 26 dollars, and in doing so the old man earned himself a temporary reprieve. Costello continues:

'As soon as I had resumed my seat at the fire a number of Portuguese soldiers entered, one of whom, taking me for a Frenchman, for I had the French soldier's jacket on, my own being wet, snapped his piece at me, which luckily hung fire. Forgetful of my wounds, I instantly rushed at him, and a regular scuffle ensued between our men and the Portuguese, until one of the latter being stabbed by a bayonet, they retired, dragging the wounded man with them. After thus ejecting the Portuguese, the victors, who had by this time got tolerably drunk, proceeded to ransack the house. Unhappily they discovered the two daughters of the old patron, who had concealed themselves upstairs. They both were young and very pretty. The mother, too, was shortly afterwards dragged from her hiding place.

'Without dwelling on the frightful scene that followed, it may be sufficient to add that our men, more infuriated by drink than before, again seized on the old man, and insisted on a fresh supply of liquor, and his protestations that he possessed no more were as vain as were all attempts to restrain them from ill-using him.'

Sickened by the horrors that were being acted around him Costello and his French prisoner left the house and entered another on the opposite side of the street. Here the troops were more peaceful but some of the troops in the house were still busy plundering it and committing the greatest outrages.

Amidst all the scenes of horror, however, there were still the odd humorous moments. Some of Badajoz's wealthier inhabitants were liberated of many of their possessions and were made to conduct them to the British camp themselves:

'. . . the conducteur was generally not only obliged to drive a herd of cattle,' wrote Grattan, 'but also to carry the bales of plunder taken by his employers – perhaps from his own house – and the stately gravity with which the Spaniard went through his work, dressed in short breeches, frilled shirt, and a hat and plumes that might vie with our eighth Henry, followed as he was by our ragamuffin soldiers with fixed bayonets, presented a scene that would puzzle even Mr Cruikshank himself to justly delineate. The plunder so captured was deposited in our camp, and placed under a guard chiefly composed of the soldiers' wives.'

The sacking of the town continued.

'Every insult, every infamy that human invention could torture into practice was committed. Age as well as youth was alike unrespected, and perhaps not one house, or one female in this vast town escaped injury: . . . the soldiers became reckless, and drank to such an excess, that no person's life, no matter of what rank, or station, or sex, was safe. If they entered a house which had not been emptied of all of its furniture or wine, they proceeded to destroy it: or, if it happened to be empty, which was generally the case, they commenced firing at the doors and windows, and not infrequently at the inmates, or at each other. They would then sally forth into the streets, and fire at the different church bells in the steeples, or the pigeons that inhabited the old Moorish turrets of the castle – even the owls were frighted from this place of refuge and, by their discordant screams, announced to their hearers the great revolution that had taken place near their once peaceful abodes. The soldiers then fired upon their own comrades, and many were killed, in endeavouring to carry away some species of plunder, by the hands of those they now so wantonly sported with; then would they turn upon the already too deeply injured females, and tear from them the trinkets that adorned their necks, fingers, or ears! And, finally, they would strip them of their wearing apparel.'

Captain Edward Hopkins, of the 4th Regiment, had taken part in the escalade of the San Vincente bastion:

'The officers had lost all command of their men in the town; those who had got drunk and had satisfied themselves with plunder congregated in small parties and fired down the streets. I saw an English soldier pass through the middle of a street with a French knapsack on his back: he received a shot through his hand from some of the drunkards at the top of the street; he merely turned round and said, "damn them, I suppose they took me for a Frenchman". An officer of the Brunswickers, who was contending with a soldier for the possession of a canary bird, was shot dead by one of these insane drunkards. Groups of soldiers were seen in all places, and could we have forgotten the distressing part of the scene, never was there such a complete masquerade. Some dressed as monks, some as friars, some in court-dresses, many carrying furniture, cloth, provisions, money, plate from the churches: the military chest was even got at.'

Young Robert Blakeney had a narrow escape whilst taking two women with the brother of one of them to St John's church, where a guard was mounted:

'. . . we were crossed by three drunken soldiers, one of whom, passing to our rear, struck the Spanish gentleman with the butt-end of his firelock on the back of his head, which nearly knocked him down. On my censuring the fellow's daring insolence in striking a person in company with two English officers, another of the men was bringing his firelock to the present, when I holloaed out loudly, "Come on quick with that guard". There was no guard near but the ruse luckily succeeded, and so quickly did the soldiers run away that I felt convinced that their apparent intoxication was feigned. On another occasion a sergeant struck me with his pike for refusing to join in plundering a family; I certainly snapped my pistol in his face, but fortunately it missed fire or he would have been killed. However, the danger which he so narrowly escaped brought him to his senses; he made an awkward apology and I considered it prudent to retire. By such means as these, by the risk and humanity of officers, many women were saved. We did not interfere with the plundering: it would have been useless.'

Surgeon Walter Henry had ridden from Campo Mayor to Badajoz on the night it was stormed. He reached the town shortly after its fall:

'I reached the bridge over the Guadiana in three-quarters of an hour, but, to my great surprise and concern, instead of finding everything quiet, and everybody occupied in attentions to the wounded, and preparations for burying the dead, as I had anticipated, I beheld a scene of the most dreadful violence and confusion. Parties of intoxicated men were roaming and reeling about, loosed from all discipline, firing into the windows, bursting open the doors, plundering, violating, shooting any person who opposed them, quarrelling about the plunder, and sometimes destroying each other.'

Indeed, the drunken British soldiers did not care who or what was shot at as they sought to find more drink and plunder. Joseph Donaldson:

'Small bands formed, and when they came to a door that offered resistance, half-a-dozen muskets were lowered at the lock, and it flew up; by this means many men were wounded, for having entered at another door, there was often a number in the house, when the door was thus blown open. The greatest number first sought the spirit stores, where having drunk an inordinate quantity, they were prepared for every sort of mischief. At one large vault in the centre of town, to which a flight of steps led, they had staved in the head of the casks and were running with their hat-caps full of it, and so much was spilt here, that some, it was said, were actually drowned in it.'

105

At seven o'clock on the morning of 7 April Lord Fitzroy Somerset crossed the bridge over to the San Christobal to call upon Governor Phillipon to surrender. He had been holding out here since the fall of the town but now felt obliged to give in and with a white handkerchief tied to a bayonet hoisted in front he and his staff, together with about a hundred soldiers, marched out to surrender. So low had the French ammunition become that the San Christobal, which was to have served as a retreat, was found to contain only thirty rounds of ammunition for cannon and not a single ration of any sort of provisions. Surgeon James McGrigor recalled seeing Phillipon shortly after his surrender:

'In one street, I met General Phillipon, the governor, with his two daughters, holding each by the hand; all three with their hair dishevelled, and with them were two British officers, each holding one of the ladies by the arm, and with their drawn swords making thrusts occasionally at soldiers who attempted to drag the ladies away. I am glad to say that these two British officers succeeded in conveying the governor and his two daughters safely through the breach, to the camp. With the exception of these ladies, I was told that very few ladies, old or young, escaped violation by our brutal soldiery, mad with brandy and with passion. At any other time, the rank and age of General Phillipon, bare-headed with his grey whiskers streaming in the wind, would have protected him from any soldiers. When I saw them pulling at these two ladies, and endeavouring to drag them away from their father, and two young officers who so gallantly defended them at the peril of their lives, I could not forbear going up, and endeavouring with threat to bring to the recollection of two soldiers of my old regiment, the 88th, how much they tarnished the glory which the Connaught Rangers had ever earned in the field, by such cowardly conduct.'

Wellington had ridden into the town with his staff on the evening of the second day and was immediately recognised by his men. 'There he comes with his long nose,' said one soldier, 'let's give him a salute,' and at that about half-a-dozen drunken British soldiers fired a volley over his head, cheering 'there goes the ol' chap who can leather the French,' and then they all ran and hid. Wellington did not take too kindly to this *feu-de-joie* and gave orders for a gallows to be erected in the square and that any man found in Badajoz the next day was to be hanged.

Costello and his French companion were making their way through the crowded streets filled with uproar and confusion when they, too, saw the Commander-in-Chief:

'In one of the streets I saw the Duke of Wellington, surrounded by a number of British soldiers, who, holding up bottles with the heads knocked off, containing wine and spirits, cried out to him, a phrase then familiarly applied to him by the men of the army, "Old boy! will you drink? The town's our own – hurrah!" In another street I observed a sort of gallows erected with three nooses hanging from them, ready for service. Johnny Castles, a man of our company, and as quiet and as inoffensive a little fellow as could be, but rather fond of a drop, but not that distilled by Jack Ketch and Co, had a near escape. He was actually brought under the gallows in a cart and the rope placed round his neck, but his life was spared. Whether this was done to frighten him or not I cannot say; but the circumstances had such an effect on him, that he took ill, and was a little deranged for some time after.'

Despite the gallows it is thought that no-one was actually hanged, although it had a sobering effect on many of the men.

At length the troops became exhausted and they began to return to the camp, carrying with them their plunder. Quartermaster William Surtees:

'Some of them had dressed themselves in priests' or friars' garments – some appeared in female dresses, as nuns, etc; and, in short, all the whimsical and fantastical figures imaginable almost were to be seen coming reeling out of the town, for by this time they were nearly all drunk. I penetrated no farther into the town that day than to a house a little beyond the breach, where I had deposited the wounded; but I saw enough in this short trip to disgust me with the doings in Badajoz at this time . . . In short, a thousand of the most tragi-comical spectacles that can possibly be imagined, might be witnessed in this devoted city.'

Joseph Donaldson thought the camp reminded him of the fairs back home:

'The camp during that day, and for some days after, was like a masquerade, the men going about intoxicated, dressed in the various dresses they had found in the town; French and Spanish officers, priests, friars and nuns, were promiscuously mixed, cutting as many antics as a montebank. It was some days before the army could be brought round to its former state of discipline. Indeed, the giving leave to plunder the town was productive of nothing but bad consequences, and for the interests of humanity, and the army at large, I hope such license may never recur, should we be again unfortunately plunged into war.'

Yet in the midst of all the chaos, debauchery and turmoil there emerged 'one of the most romantic tales of love and war that have ever been set down on paper'. The day after the storm, Kincaid was talking with a friend at the door of his tent when two young ladies came hurrying towards them from the town. As they approached the elder of the two threw back her mantilla and began to address them. She said her husband was a Spanish officer and that yesterday she and her younger sister were living in a fine house in the town, but today she had nowhere to go and nothing to eat. She said her house was a wreck and they had both been assaulted by British soldiers – the blood was still trickling down their necks, caused by the wrenching of their ear-rings from their ears. She cared little for herself but she wanted to find security for her younger sister and had no choice but to throw themselves upon the protection of any British officer who would afford it. Kincaid fell in love with the young girl at once:

'Fourteen summers had not yet passed over her youthful countenance, which was of a delicate freshness – more English than Spanish; her face, though not perhaps rigidly beautiful, was nevertheless so remarkably handsome, and so irresistibly attractive, surmounting a figure cast in nature's fairest mould, that to look at her was to love her; and I did love her; but I never told my love, and in the meantime another and more impudent fellow stepped in and won her! But yet I was happy, for in him she found such a one as her loveliness and her misfortune claimed – a man of honour, and a husband in every way worthy of her!'

The 'impudent fellow' who had stepped in was Harry Smith, and three days afterwards he and his bride, Juana Maria de Los Dolores de Leon, were married in the presence of Wellington, who himself gave away the bride. Juana proved to be a faithful wife and companion to her husband and together they travelled many a distant campaign in Spain, Belgium, India and South Africa, herself being the Lady Smith who gave her name to the town where, ninety years later, another of history's great sieges took place. But theirs is another story.

Back inside Badajoz Edward Costello and his French companion had sat down to rest by the bridge leading to the San Christobal. They had not been seated long when they found themselves being entertained by a large baboon that was being tormented by a party of British soldiers:

'The poor animal had been wounded in the foot, probably by one of our men, and by his chattering, grinning, and droll gesticulations, he showed as much aversion to the red coats as any of the French could possibly have done. While the men continued teasing the animal, a sergeant, stating that it belonged to the Colonel of the 4th Regiment, who he said was wounded, attempted to take the beast away whereupon the party being divided in their sentiments, a scuffle ensued, in which several men were wounded with bayonets.

'As we got up to proceed, we saw a number of Frenchmen guarded by our soldiers, coming over the bridge. They were the prisoners taken in the Fort San Christobal, which but an hour or two previously had surrendered. These were soon surrounded by our men, who began examining their knapsacks, from whence a number of watches, dollars, etc, were quickly extracted . . . we pursued our way until near the gates that led to the camp, when rather an affecting scene came under my eye. A little fellow, a drummer boy belonging to the 88th Regiment, was lying wounded and crying bitterly, his leg being broken by a shot. On telling him I would get him carried by the Frenchman, if he wished, "Oh no!" said the boy, "I don't

Juana Maria de Los Dolores de Leon, afterwards Lady Smith.

care for myself. Look at my poor father, where he lies!" pointing to a man shot through the head, lying weltering in a gore of blood. Poor little fellow! I gave him a couple of dollars, and called some men to his assistance, when I was compelled to leave him. We soon arrived at the camp ground of the 3rd Division. I dismounted and while sitting on one of the men's knapsacks, a soldier of the 83rd Regiment was engaged in cleaning his firelock, when the piece went off and shot a corporal through the head, wounding also the hand of another man.'

Eventually Costello left the town and returned to the camp where he

109

had to part with his French companion, who was sent to join the other French prisoners.

As the British troops began to exhaust themselves, Wellington thought it possible to restore order and on 7 April he issued an order that it was high time for the plunder to cease. On 8 April the Marshal Provost marched into the town with Power's Portuguese brigade who would form the garrison. These latter troops, however, proved to be just as bad as those already in the town and therefore on 9 April Power's brigade were kept under arms all day until order was finally restored, and the stragglers at last driven out back to the camp. It has often been said, however, that the disorder 'subsided rather than was quelled'.

When the troops were brought under order it was possible to begin to attend to the wounded. The sights at the breaches, and at those places where the fighting had been particularly violent, presented to those who witnessed them something which they had never before experienced nor ever would again. Walter Henry was shocked when he saw the awful scene in the main breach:

'There lay a frightful heap of fourteen or 1,500 British soldiers, many dead but still warm, mixed with the desperately wounded, to whom no assistance could be given. There lay the burned and blackened corpses of those that had perished by the explosions, mixed with those that were torn to pieces by round shot or grape, and killed by musketry, stiffening in their gore, body piled upon body, involved and intermixed into one hideous and enormous mass of carnage; whilst the morning sunbeams, falling on this awful pile, seemed to my imagination pale and lugubrious as during an eclipse.

'At the foot of the castle wall, where the 3rd Division had escaladed, the dead lay thick, and a great number were to be seen about the San Vincente bastion at the opposite side of the works. A number had been drowned in the cunette of the ditch, near the Trinidad bastion, but the chief slaughter had taken place at the great breach. There stood still the terrific beam across the top, armed with its sharp and bristling sword blades, which no human dexterity or strength could pass without impalement. The smell of burned flesh was yet shockingly strong and disgusting.'

Quartermaster Surtees had gone down to the town at daylight the morning after the storm with his commanding officer, Captain Percival:

'... and now he and I, hearing the heart-piercing and affecting groans which arose from the numbers of wounded still lying in the ditch, set to work to get as many of these poor fellows removed as was in our power. This we found a most arduous and difficult undertaking, as we could not do it without the aid of a considerable number of men; and it was a work of danger to attempt to force the now lawless soldiers to obey, and stop with us till this work of necessity and humanity was accomplished.

'All thought of what they owed their wounded comrades, and of the

110

probability that ere long a similar fate might be their own, was swallowed up in their abominable rage for drink and plunder; however, by perseverance, and occasionally using his stick, my commandant at length compelled a few fellows to lend their assistance in removing what we could into the town. But this was a most heart-rending duty, for, from the innumerable cries of – "Oh! for God's sake, come and remove me!" it was difficult to select the most proper objects for such care. Those who appeared likely to die, of course, it would have been but cruelty to put them to the pain of a removal: and many who, from the nature of their wounds, required great care and attention in carrying them, the half-drunken brutes whom we were forced to employ exceedingly tortured and injured; nay, in carrying one man out of the ditch they very frequently kicked or trod upon several others, whom to touch was like death to them, and which produced the most agonising cries imaginable.'

Soldiers wandered amongst the dead and dying looking for their friends or relatives. George Simons:

'I saw my poor friend Major O'Hare lying dead upon the breach. Two or three musket balls had passed through his breast. A gallant fellow, Sergeant Flemming, was also dead by his side, a man who had always been with him. I called to rememberance poor O'Hare's last words before he marched off to lead the advance. He shook me by the hand saying, "A Lieutenant-Colonel or cold meat in a few hours." I was now gazing upon his body lying stretched and naked amongst thousands more.'

By now the sun had grown hot and the heat of the sun and the very unpleasant effluvia which rose from the dead and wounded caused the work of removing the wounded to be stopped, at least for a while. Although a great many had been removed a greater number still remained, groaning in the ditch. The soldiers helping were not very useful, most of them being still half-drunk and doing more harm than good.

William Surtees found his messmate, Cary, lying beneath one of the ladders in the ditch:

'He was shot through the head, and I doubt not received his death-wound on the ladder, from which in all probability he fell. He was stripped completely naked, save a flannel waistcoat which he wore next to his skin. I had him taken up and placed upon a shutter, (he still breathed a little, though quite insensible) and carried him to the camp. A sergeant and some men, whom we had pressed to carry him, were so drunk that they let him fall from off their shoulders, and his body fell with great force to the ground. I shuddered, but poor Cary, I believe, was past all feeling, or the fall would have greatly injured him. We laid him in his tent, but it was not long ere my kind, esteemed, and lamented friend breathed his last.'

On the third day after the fall of the town, Kincaid and his comrade, Colonel Cameron, rode over to the Guadiana in order to take a bath:

'. . . and, in passing the verge of the camp of the 5th Division, we saw two soldiers standing at the door of a small shed, or outhouse, shouting, waving their caps, and making signs that they wanted to speak to us. We rode up to see what they wanted, and found that the poor fellows had each lost a leg. They told us that a surgeon had dressed their wounds on the night of the assault, but that they had ever since been without food or assistance of any kind, although they, each day, had opportunities of soliciting the aid of many of their comrades, from whom they could obtain nothing but promises. In short, surrounded by thousands of their countrymen within call, and not more than 300 yards from their own regiment, they were unable to interest any one on their behalf, and were literally starving. It is unnecessary to say that we instantly galloped back to the camp and had them removed to the hospital.'

Costello remained in the camp for three days before he could be moved to a hospital in Badajoz:

'during which I had an opportunity of hearing of the casualties that occurred. The number of men killed, wounded, and absent was such, that the company could not muster a dozen men on parade for three days afterwards. Parties were to be sent to the breaches to bury the dead, which now began to smell most dreadfully; but we could not collect men enough to perform that duty. My poor old captain, Major O'Hare, was amongst the slain, and had not less than ten or a dozen balls through his body.'

The noise and the outrageous behaviour of the troops had sickened Joseph Donaldson, who made his way from the town to the breaches. Here was a contrast indeed:

'Here all was comparatively silent, unless here and there a groan from the poor fellows who lay wounded, and who were unable to move. As I looked round, several voices assailed my ear begging for a drink of water; I went, and having filled a large pitcher which I found, relieved their wants as far as I could.

'When I observed the defences that had been made here, I could not wonder at our troops not succeeding in the assault. The ascent of the breach near the top was covered with planks of wood firmly connected together, staked down, and stuck full of sword and bayonet blades, which were firmly fastened into the wood with the points up; round the breach a deep trench was cut in the ramparts, which was planted full of muskets with the bayonets fixed in the earth up to the locks. Exclusive of this they had shell and hand grenades ready loaded, piled on the ramparts, which they lighted and threw down amongst the assailants. Round this place death appeared in every form, the whole ascent was completely covered with the killed, and for many yards around the approach to the walls, with every variety of expression in their countenance, from calm placidity to the greatest agony. Anxious to see the place where we had so severe a struggle the preceding night, I bent my steps to the ditch where we had placed the ladders to escalade the castle. The sight here was enough to harrow up the soul, and of which no description of mine could convey an idea. Beneath

112

one of the ladders, amongst others, lay a corporal of the 45th Regiment, who, when wounded, had fallen forward on his knees and hands, and the foot of the ladder had been, in the confusion, placed on his back. Whether the wound would have been mortal, I do not know, but the weight of the men ascending the ladder had facilitated his death, for the blood was forced out of his ears, mouth, and nose.'

Robert Blakeney described the scene:

'When I arrived at the great breach, the inundation presented an awful contrast to the silvery Guadiana; it was fairly stained with gore, which through the vivid reflection of the brilliant sun, whose glowing heat already drew the watery vapours from its surface, gave it the appearance of a fiery lake of smoking blood, in which were seen the bodies of many a gallant British soldier. The ditches were strewn with killed and wounded; but the approach to the bottom of the main breach was fairly choked with dead. A row of chevaux-de-frise, armed with sword blades, barred the entrance at the top of the breach and so firmly fixed that when the 4th and Light Divisions marched through, the greatest exertion was required to make a sufficient opening for their admittance. Boards fastened with ropes to plugs driven into the ground within the ramparts were let down, and covered nearly the whole surface of the breach; these boards were so thickly studded with sharp pointed spikes that one could not introduce a hand between them; they did not stick out at right angles to the board, but were all slanting upwards. In rear of the chevaux-de-frise the ramparts had deep cuts in all directions, like a tanyard, so that it required light to enable one to move safely through them, even were there no opposing enemy. From the number of muskets found close behind the breach, all the men who could possibly be brought together in so small a place must have had at least twenty firelocks each, no doubt kept continually loaded by persons in the rear. Two British soldiers only entered the main breach during the assault; I saw both their bodies. If any others entered they must have been thrown back over the walls, for it is certain that at dawn of 7 April no more than two British bodies were within the walls near the main breach. In the Santa Maria breach not one had entered. At the foot of this breach the same sickening sight appeared as at that of Trinidad: numberless dead were strewn around the place. On looking down these breaches, I recognised many old friends, whose society I had enjoyed a few hours before, now lying stiff in death.'

Charles Von Hodenberg's description of the horrors of Badajoz was written two days after the storm:

'I was one of the first of the idle spectators who went into the town, when daylight appeared, and the firing had nearly ceased. I closely viewed the breaches, which were no more than part of the exterior wall battered down, which, with the rubbish and some soil of the rampart, had tumbled into the ditch, so as to make the ascent a little less than perpendicular. I found it difficult to climb up, and was struck with astonishment and admiration at

A scene in Badajoz after the storming of the town.

the supernatural bravery and coolness that had been evinced by our men. In some parts they had, when descending into the ditch, found themselves up to the neck in water, which the enemy had let in from the river. This alone, on a dark night, and under a most destructive fire, might have checked less brave soldiers. They had pushed on to the breaches, and forcing their way to the top, found them guarded with chevaux-de-frise of sharpened sword blades carefully chained together, so that it required time and unusual effort to remove them.

'Behind had stood the enemy, twelve deep, keeping up a steady fire until our men had come up to the very muzzles of their muskets. I counted between 700–800 of our dead, among them several friends and acquaintances with whom I had conversed on the previous day, and who had told me with much cheerfulness what part was allowed to each of them in the attack. I regret to say that of the wounded – who had been about 2,000 – many were still lying on the rampart or in the ditch, still without assistance.'

John Cooke also examined the breaches by day. He thought the defences to be impregnable and found it difficult to pass over the chevaux-de-frise even in daytime:

'One man only was at the top of the left breach (the heaps of dead had, as a matter of course, rolled to the bottom) and that was one of the 95th Rifles, who had succeeded in getting his head under the chevaux-de-frise, which was battered to pieces, and his arms and shoulders torn asunder with bayonet wounds . . . Poor McLeod, in his 27th year, was buried half-a-mile from the town, on the south side, opposite our camp, on the slope of a hill. We did not like to take him to the miserable breach, where, from the warmth of the weather, the dead soldiers had begun to turn, and their blackened bodies had swollen enormously; we therefore laid him amongst some young springing corn, and, with sorrowful hearts, six of us (all that remained of the officers able to stand) saw him covered in the earth. His cap, all muddy, was handed to me, being without one, with merely a hand-kerchief round my bruised head, one eye closed, and also a slight wound in my head.

'The country was open. The dead, the dying, and the wounded, were scattered abroad: some in tents, others exposed to the sun by day, and the heavy dew by night. At length, with considerable difficulty, I found my friend Madden, lying in a tent, with his trousers on and his shirt off, covered with blood, and bandaged across the body to support his broken shoulder, laid on his back, and unable to move. He asked for his brother – "Why does he not come to see me?" I turned my head away; for his gallant young brother (a captain of the 52nd) was amongst the slain.'

In all, the capture of Badajoz cost Wellington 5,000 men and officers, and of these almost 3,000 men had become casualties during the assault. Five generals, Kempt, Harvey, Bowes, Colville and Picton were wounded. The 3rd Division lost about 500 men whilst esca-lading the castle and the 5th Division about the same at the San Vincente, whilst at the breaches the 4th and Light Divisions suf-fered almost 1,000 casualties. Let Napier have the last word on the aftermath of the storming:

'Let any man picture to himself this frightful scene of carnage taking place in a space of less than a hundred square yards. Let him consider that the slain died not all suddenly, nor by one manner of death; that some perished by steel, some by shot, some by water, that some were crushed and mangled by heavy weights, some trampled upon, some dashed to atoms by the fiery explosions; that for hours this destruction was endured without shrinking, and that the town was won at last, let any man consider this and he must admit that a British army bears with it an awful power.'

6

Epilogue

The fall of Badajoz came as a complete shock to the French who had complete confidence in the garrison's ability to withstand Wellington's assaults until relief could be got through to them. General Léry, Engineer in Chief to the Army of the South, wrote to General Kellerman:

'The fall of Badajoz cost me eight engineers. I am not yet acquainted with the details of that fatal event. Never was there a place in a better state, better supplied, or better provided with the requisite number of troops. There is in that event a marked fatality. I confess my inability to account for its inadequate defence. Very extensive works have been constructed. All our calculations have been disappointed. The army of Portugal withdrew to a greater distance when it should have drawn nearer; and thus Lord Wellington has taken the place, as it were, in the presence of two armies, amounting together to about 80,000 men. This is the consequence of the want of a supreme chief. In short, I think the capture of Badajoz a very extraordinary event; and I should be much at a loss to account for it in any manner consistent with probability.'

Although Léry states that he was not yet in possession of the full details of the siege when he wrote to Kellerman, his views are nevertheless a little unfair to Phillipon and his garrison. After all, it was not his fault that the two armies of Marmont and Soult should let themselves be sidetracked into fighting pointless actions against local Spanish units instead of proceeding directly to relieve Badajoz. Moreover, Phillipon proved to be a master of defence and organised his men so well that they inflicted such fearful losses on the British troops that even Wellington was said to have broken down when he saw the cream of his army smashed on the defences in the breaches. In a letter to Lord Liverpool he wrote:

'The capture of Badajoz affords as strong an instance of the gallantry of our troops as has ever been displayed. But I anxiously hope that I shall never again be the instrument of putting them to such a test as that to which they were put last night. I assure your lordship that it is quite impossible to carry fortified places by *vive force* without incurring great loss, and being exposed to the chance of failure unless the army should be provided with a sufficient trained corps of sappers and miners . . . the consequence of being so unprovided with the people necessary to approach a regularly fortified place are, first, our engineers, though well educated and brave, have never turned their minds to the mode of conducting a regular siege, as it is useless to think of that which is impossible, in our service, to perform. They think they have done their duty when they have constructed a battery with a secure communication to it, which can breach the place. Secondly, these breaches have to be carried by *vive force*, at an infinite sacrifice of officers and soldiers . . . These great losses could be avoided, and, in my opinion, time gained in every siege, if we had properly trained people to carry it on. I declare that I have never seen breaches more practicable in themselves than the three in the walls of Badajoz, and the fortress must have surrendered with these breaches open, if I had been able to "approach" the place. But when I made the third breach on the evening of the 6 April, I could do no more. I was then obliged either to storm or to give the business up, and when I ordered the assault I was certain that I should lose our best officers and men. It is a cruel situation for any person to be placed in, and I earnestly recommend to your lordship to have a corps of sappers and miners formed without loss of time.'

Wellington followed this up with another letter, this time addressed to the Lieutenant-Colonel Torrens, military secretary to the King, and dated the day after the storming, in which he says:

'Our loss has been very great . . . The truth is, that equipped as we are, the British army are not capable of carrying on a regular siege.'

In response to Wellington's complaints a warrant was issued for the purpose of creating the Royal Corps of Sappers and Miners. This was issued on 23 April, seventeen days after the storming of Badajoz but it was still not until the siege of San Sebastian, the following year, that they were really made any use of and even then their numbers were woefully inadequate.

However, Badajoz was in British hands and it remained so for the rest of the war, which Wellington brought to a successful conclusion two years and many great victories later.

As for Governor Armand Phillipon, he was taken prisoner to England but managed to escape to France, where he rejoined the army and saw action in Russia and Germany, fighting under Vandamme at Kulm, in August 1813. In September of the same year he retired from active service and was later reconciled with the Bourbons.

In spite of their dreadful behaviour afterwards, the storming of Badajoz will remain forever as an outstanding example of the courage and determination of the British soldiers. There would be greater battles to be fought in the Peninsular, and more famous battles later on, like Waterloo, but for those who took part and survived it would be the name of Badajoz that would stir chilling memories of what was, for the British army, the most violent and horrific episode of their campaign in the Peninsular.

Badajoz Today

It is very easy to read how the British troops at Badajoz climbed the walls of the town to victory, but when one actually sees just how formidable the walls really are it is only then that one appreciates the full magnitude of their achievements on that April night.

Large stretches of the walls still exist today in Badajoz, although tall trees have grown up, partially hiding certain portions from view. The high, grey walls of the San Vincente bastion are unchanged and gazing up at them one wonders how on earth Leith's men managed to climb them. The breaches were repaired, although today a road passes through the breach made in the curtain between the Santa Maria and La Trinidad bastions. The ditch has gone, replaced by neatly laid gardens and whilst on a visit there I watched a young couple, newly married, stroll through them looking for a shady spot to pose for their wedding photographs. How different a scene from the carnage in 1812. The area covering the approaches to the breaches has also disappeared beneath a multitude of shabby-looking buildings and a bull-ring.

The Castle is virtually unchanged and here it is easier to visualise the events that took place during the storming. Again, one can only wonder at the bravery of the British troops. The Castle is perched at the top of a steep hill which represents quite a climb in itself, let alone having to climb the walls at the top of it, all the time under a hail of fire. Many trees have since grown up but apart from that it has changed little. One can stand on the Castle ramparts and appreciate just how great an advantage the French defenders had over Picton's men at this point and then wonder how the British troops ever got inside. It is also possible from here to gaze down at the Rivellas, still flowing at the foot of the hill where the frogs continue to croak, and then out into the fields beyond, where the extreme right of the British trenches were situated.

The San Roque remains in part today where the Rivellas was dammed. The Tête du Pont also remains, sited on the opposite side of the river Guadiana which flows beneath the old Roman bridge. The San Christobal, where Phillipon surrendered, stands high on the hill opposite Badajoz, as easy to defend now as it was in 1812.

The town itself has changed with the times, of course, but it is easy to imagine the chaos which followed the storming in the small and narrow cobbled streets that still cover a large part of Badajoz today.

Visitors to the town will find no memorials to Wellington's men and one feels that the events of 6 April 1812 are now just bad but distant memories which are slowly fading into the past, along with the ghosts of all those British soldiers who made it to hell before daylight.

Appendix I

Anglo-Portuguese Losses at Badajoz 1812

Assault

British Loss

	Killed	Wounded
Generals	—	5
Staff	1	11

	Officers	Soldiers
Artillery	2	20
Engineers	5	5
Total	7	25

Light division

	Officers	Soldiers	Total
43rd	18	329	347
52nd	18	305	323
95th 1st Bat	14	179	193
95th 3rd Bat	8	56	64
Total	58	869	927

Third division

	Officers	Soldiers	Total
5th	4	41	45
45th	14	83	97
74th	7	47	54
77th	3	10	13
83rd	8	62	70
88th	10	135	145
94th	2	154	156
Total	48	532	580

Fourth division

	Officers	Soldiers	Total
7th	17	163	180
23rd	17	134	151
27th	15	170	185
40th	16	124	140
48th	19	154	173
Total	84	745	829

Fifth division

	Officers	Soldiers	Total
1st	2	—	2
4th	17	213	230
9th	—	—	—
30th	6	126	132
38th	5	37	42
44th	9	95	104
Total	39	471	510
60th*	4	30	34
Brunswick Oels*	2	33	35

Total British loss at the assault

Officers	Sergeants	Soldiers	
51	40	560	killed
213	153	1983	wounded
—	1	21	missing
			Total 3022

Total Portuguese loss at the assault

8	6	141	killed
45	32	468	wounded
—	—	30	missing
			Total 730

Grand Total

317	232	3203	3752

*These regiments were attached by companies to the third, fourth and fifth divisions.

Appendix II

The Garrison in Badajoz, 16 March 1812

État-Major:

Le baron Phillipon, général de division,
    governeur
Duhamel, lieutenant, aide-de-camp
Desmeuve, lieutenant, aide-de-camp
Le baron Veiland, général de brigade,
    commandant en second
Massot, capitaine, aide-de-camp
Saint-Vincent, lieutenant, aide-de-camp
Le chevalier Charpentier, major commandant
    de la place
De Grasse, capitaine d'état-major
Denisot, lieutenant d'état-major
Gaspard Thierry, colonel d'état-major
Pineau, colonel d'état-major

                          Total 11

Artillerie:

Picoteau, colonel directeur
L'Espagnol, chef de bataillon
Quirot, capitaine
D'André Saint-Victor, capitaine
Dubois, capitaine
Rio, chef de bataillon (Espagnol)
Horre, capitaine (Espagnol)

                          Total 7

Genie:

Lamare, colonel, directeur des fortifications
Truilhier, chef de bataillon
Lefaivre, capitaine
Meynhart, capitaine
Lenoir, capitaine de mineurs
Mailhet, lieutenant
Martin, capitaine de sapeurs
Vallon, lieutenant
Henneberg, adjudant

                          Total 9

Administrations:

Pasius, sous-inspecteur aux revues
Vienné, commissaire des guerres
L.Coupin, garde-magasin
Estruc, médecin
Lacipierre, chirurgien-major
Malcuisant, aide-major
Becard, chirurgien

Total 7

Troupes:

Artillerie: Officiers compris: la 12th compagnie du 1st regiment; la 1st compagnie du 5th regiment; et un détachement d'ouvriers de la 4th compagnie

Total 233

Genie: Officiers compris: 2nd compagnie du 2nd bataillon de mineurs; 1st compagnie du 2nd bataillon de sapeurs; et un détachement de la 5th compagnie du même bataillon

Total 263

Cavalerie: Dragons et Chasseurs a cheval, deux officiers compris   Total 50

Infanterie: Officiers compris: 9th leger, 3rd bataillon; 28th, 3rd bataillon; 58th de ligne, 1st bataillon; 88th de ligne, 3rd bataillon; 103rd de ligne, 3rd bataillon; et un détachement du 64th de ligne

Total 2673

Un régiment du Hesse-Darmstadt, avec un détachement de canonniers, officiers compris
Total 900

Un détachement espagnol, officiers compris
Total 50

Train d'artillerie et équipage militaires,
environ   Total 130

Employés des administrations, cantiniers, marchands, malades et domestiques
Total 667

Total Combatants 4333

Total General 5000

Loss in killed and wounded, about 1,500
Prisoners of war, officers included 3,500

Appendix III

Return of Killed and Wounded Officers

of the Army under the command of His Excellency General The Earl of Wellington, at the storming of Badajoz, 6 to 7 April 1812

Officers Killed:

Artillery	Capt. Latham
Engineers	Lts. Lacelles, De Salubury
1/4 Reg.	Capt. Bellingham; Lieut. Stavely
2/5 Reg.	Maj. Ridge
1/7 Reg.	Maj. Singer; Capt. Cholwick; Lts. Ray, Fowler, Pike
1/23 Reg.	Capt. Maw; Lt. Collins
3/27 Reg.	Capt. Jones; Lts. Levinge, Simcoe, Whyte
23 Reg.	Capt. Johnson, A.D.C. to Maj-Gen. Bowes
2/38 Reg.	Ens. Evans
1/40 Reg.	Lts. Greenshields, Ayling; Volun. O'Brien
42 Reg.	Capt. Monro
1/43 Reg.	Lt-Col. Mcleod; Lts. Harvest, Taggart
2/44 Reg.	Lts. Unthank, Argent
1/45 Reg.	Capt. Herrick; Ens. McDonnell, Collins
1/48 Reg.	Capt. Brooke; Lt. Chiliot, Ens. Barker
1/52 Reg.	Capts. Jones, Madden, Poole; Lts. Booth, Royle
5/60 Reg.	Lt. Sterne
2/83 Reg.	Capt. Fry
1/88 Reg.	Capt. Lindsey; Lts. Mansfield, McAlpin
94 Reg.	Ens. Long
1/95 Reg.	Maj. O'Hare; Capt. Diggle; Lt. Stokes
3/95 Reg.	Lts. Hovenden, Cary, Allex, Cromdace

Portuguese

3rd line	Lt. de Silviera
11th line	Lt. McDonnell (91st British)
23rd line	Ens. de Cavallo
1st Cac.	Lt. St Valez
3rd Cac.	Capt. Morphew (R.W.I.R. British)
8th Cac.	Capt. Bunting (Y.L.I. British); Lt. Pinta de Lousac

Wounded

General Staff

77 Reg.	Lt-Gen. Sir Thomas Picton; Maj-Gen. Hon. C. Colville
81 Reg.	Maj-Gen. Kempt
50 Reg.	Maj-Gen. Walker
6 Reg.	Maj-Gen. Bowes
7 Reg.	Maj.Hon. H. Packenham, asst. adj.gen.; Majs. Brooke, Perm
81 Reg.	Capt. James, D.ass.adj.gen.
92 Reg.	Brig.Maj. McPherson
28 Reg.	Brig.Maj. Potter
45 Reg.	Brig.Maj. Campbell
30 Reg.	Brig.Maj. Machell
71 Reg.	Capt. Spottiswoode, A.D.C. to Maj-Gen. Colville
5 Reg.	Capt. Bennet, A.D.C. to Gen. Kempt
50 Reg.	Lt. Johnstone, A.D.C. to Gen. Walker
R.Eng.	Capts. Nicholas, Williams; Lt. Emmett
K.G.A.	Lt. Gochen
I Royal	Lts. Rae, McNail, acting engineers
1/4 Reg.	Maj. Faunce; Capts. Williamson, Wilson, Burke, Hanwell; Lts. Salvin, Convey, Boyd, Dean, Brown, Sheppard, Craster, Aley; Ens. Rawlins, Arnold
2/5 Reg.	Capt. Doyle; Lt. Pennington; Ens. Hopkins
1/7 Reg.	Lt-Col. Blakeney; Capt. Mair; Lts. St Pol, Moses, Devey, Barrington, Lester, Russell, George, Henry, Baldwin, Knowles
1/23 Reg.	Capts. Leckey, Stainforth, Hawtyn; Lts. Johnson, Harrison, Tucker, G. Brown, Farmer, Walker, Brownson, Fielding, Whaley, Holmes, Winyates, Llewelyn
3/27 Reg.	Maj. Erskine; Capt. Ward; Lts. Thompson,Ratcliffe, Gordon, Moore, Hanbey, Pollock, Weir; Adj. Davidson; Ens. Warrington
2/30 Reg.	Maj. Grey; Capts. Hitchin, Chambers; Lts. Baillie, Neville, Pratt
2/38 Reg.	Capt. Barnard; Lts. Magill, Lawrence; Ens. Reed
1/40 Reg.	Lt-Col. Harcourt; Maj. Gillies; Capts. Phillips,Bowen; Lts. Street, Grey, Moore, Turton, Butler, Millar, Anthony, Toole, Gorman; Ens. Johnson; Volun. Widenham
1/43 Reg.	Maj. Wells; Capts. Ferguson, Stroud; Lts. Pollock, Rideout, Capell, W. Freer, Oglander, Madden, E. Freer, Consadine, Bailie, Hodgson, O'Connell, Cook
2/44 Reg.	Lt-Col. H. G. Carlton; Capts. Berwick, Brugh, Jervoise; Lts. Mead, Sinclair; Ens. O'Reilly
1/45 Reg.	Capts. Lightfoot, Flaharty; Lts. Powell, Reynett, Metcalfe, MacPherson, Dale, Monroe; Ens. Jones, Stewart; Volun. Percy

1/48 Reg.	Lt-Col. Erskine; Maj. Wilson; Capts. Bell, Turnpenny, French; Lts. Brook, Stroud, Cuthbertson, Robinson, Armstrong, Wilson, Pountney; Ens. Thatcher, Johnson, Bourke, Thompson
1/50 Reg.	Lt. MacCarthy, ass.eng.
1/52 Reg.	Lt-Col. Gibbs; Maj. Mein; Capts. R. Campbell, Merry; Lts. McNair, Kinlock, York, Davis, Royds, Blackwood, Barlow, C. Dawson; Ens. Gawler; adj. Winterbottom
5/60 Reg.	Lt-Cols. Williams, Fitzgerald; Lts. Gilse, Broety
74 Reg.	Lt-Col. Hon. P. French; Capts. Langlands, Thompson; Lts. Grant, King, Pattison, Ironside
77 Reg.	Lt-Col. Duncan; Lts. Clarke, Pennefather; Adj. Jones
2/83 Reg.	Lts. Bowles, O'Neil, Bloomfield, Barry, Fitzgibbon; Ens. Vavasour, Lane; Volun. Illera
1/88 Reg.	Capts. Murphy, Peshall; Lts. Davern, Cockburn, Whitelaw, Stewart; Ens. Grattan
92 Reg.	Lt. Cattenhaugh, acting eng.
94 Reg.	Lt. Bogue
1/95 Reg.	Capts. Crampton, Balvaired, Grey, McDermid; Lts. Johnson, Gardiner, Manners, McPherson, Forster, Fitzmaurice
3/95 Reg.	Lts. McDonald, Worsley, Stewart, Farmer; Volun. Lawson
Brunsk.	Capt. Girswald; Lt. Kunowskey
Portug.	Brig-Gen. Harvey (79 Brit.); Capt. Peacock (44 Brit); Lt. Alvaro di Costa, A.D.C. to Gen. Harvey; Majs. Tullock (Brit. Art.), Anderson (42 Brit.); Capts. J. de Mattos, F. de Almeida, J. Maria; Lts. de la Serda, Clements, Pinto, dos Santos, Cebral; Ens. Gonoon, Tavary, Oliva, d'Alverida; Gos.Bernido
15 Reg.	Capt. T. O'Neil (32 Brit.); Ens. Poulal
21 Reg.	Lt. Peruva
23 Reg.	Capt. R. Felix; Lts. Rebocho, Madieras; Ens. Mendorca, Pedro Retocho, Servieca
Caca. I	Maj. Algeo (34 Brit.); Capt. MacDonald (71 Brit.); Ens. Rebello
Caca. 3	Lt-Col. Elder (95 Brit.); Maj. de Selviera; Capts. Ignacio, Dobbin, (27 Brit.); Lts. Paxato, D'Ainderido
Caca. 6	Capt. O'Hara (47 Brit.); Lts. Cavmancho, Graves; Ens. Jose de Almeida
Caca. 8	Capt. Magelaens; Lt. Condose; Ens. Lecha

Total loss from 18 to 26 March:
9 Officers; 5 sergeants; 1 drummer; 114 rank and file killed; 34 Officers; 20 sergeants; 2 drummers; 530 rank and file wounded; 1 rank and file missing.

Appendix IV

Badajoz

Thanks to General the Earl of Wellington, and other officers, for the Military Skill and Professional Ability displayed by them at the Siege of Badajoz.

House of Commons – lunae, 27 die Aprilis 1812

The Army

Resolved, Nemine Contradicente, That the Thanks of this House be given to General the Earl of Wellington, for the great ability and military skill manifested by him in the recent Siege of Badajoz, by which that important Fortress has been wrested from the possession of the Enemy.

Resolved, Nemine Contradicente, That the Thanks of this House be given to Lieutenant-General Sir William Carr Beresford, Knight of the Most honourable Order of the Bath, Lieutenant-General James Leith, Lieutenant-General Thomas Picton, Major-General the Honourable Charles Stewart, Major-General the Honourable Charles Colville, Major-General Barnard Ford Bowes, Major-General Andrew Hay, Major-General George Townsend Walker, and Major-General James Kempt, and likewise to Brigadier-General William Maundy Harvey, Brigadier-General Champlemond, and Brigadier Manley Power, of the Portuguese Service, for their distinguished exertions during the recent Siege of Badajoz, which was so gloriously terminated by the successful assault of that important Fortress in the night of the 6th instant.

Resolved, Neminde Contradicente, That the Thanks of this House be given to the Officers belonging to the Corps of Royal Engineers, and to the Royal Artillery and Portuguese Artillery, serving under the command of the Earl of Wellington at the recent Siege of Badajoz, for the professional ability, ardour and indefatigable zeal displayed by them throughout that arduous operation.

Resolved, Nemine Contradicente, That the Thanks of this House be given to the Officers of the British and Portuguese Forces employed in the recent Siege of Badajoz, for the valour, zeal and ability displayed by them throughout that arduous operation, and particularly in the glorious capture of the place by assault in the night of the 6th instant.

Resolved, Nemine Contradicente, That this House doth highly acknowledge, and approve of, the distinguished bravery, zeal and discipline manifested by the Non-commissioned Officers and Soldiers of the British and Portuguese Forces employed in the recent Siege of Badajoz, and particularly in the glorious capture of that place by assault in the night of the 6th instant.

Ordered, that Mr Speaker do transmit the said Resolutions to General the Earl of Wellington, and that his Lordship be desired to communicate the same to the Generals and Allied Armies employed in the late Siege and Capture of Badajoz.

Glossary of Siege Terms

Artillery Park The place chosen by the besieging commander where he holds his reserve artillery, his ammunition and supplies and materials until they are ready for use.

Bastion These bastions were strongholds which, when linked together, formed an enclosure around a town or city. The outward pointing angle of a bastion was formed by the conjunction of two walls.

Battery A gun position, laid with planks to prevent the wheels of the guns and the carriages from sinking into the ground. A sunken battery is laid deep in the earth.

Blinds Wooden frames fixed together and placed upright in the ground against the sides of saps in order to sustain the the earth. Also used to protect troops from stones or grenades when lain across the tops of the saps and covered with fascines.

Breach An opening made in the wall or rampart of a fortified place, either by a mine or cannon.

Chevaux-de-frise Formed of large pieces of timber stuck full of spikes, sword blades or long nails. These are used to block up breaches and to prevent entry by enemy troops.

Counterguard A work usually placed before a ravelin or bastion and has its sides parallel to them.

Covered Way A broad way left beyond the counterscarp and which goes all the way round the works of a fortified place. Usually protected by a parapet.

Crown Work A kind of hornwork with a ditch and a rampart. Like the other works, it is used to cover an area of ground or to secure some rising ground from the enemy, e.g. Pardaleras.

Curtain The curtain is the wall which joins together two bastions.

Ditch The ditch is a hollow channel made beyond the rampart and goes all the way around the place. The edges of the ditch are made sloping with the slope nearest the place called the scarp and the slope nearest the besiegers called the counterscarp.

Embrasures Openings made in fortifications through which guns or muskets are fired.

Fascines Composed of bundles of branches like faggots, six feet long and tied in two places. Used to strengthen or replace the walls of trenches or other works.

Forlorn Hope Small group of forty men and an officer, all eager volunteers, who preceded the storming parties during the assault.

Gabions A kind of basket, about three feet high and usually of the same diameter. Filled with earth it was used to provide cover during the siege.

Glacis The ground beyond the covered way, sloping from the top of the parapet to the level ground.

Gorge The part of the work next to the body of the place where there is no parapet or rampart.

Hornwork Placed before a ravelin, pointing towards the besiegers, and used to protect the ravelin and the curtain.

Lodgment A kind of trench made in a work after the enemy have been driven from it. Used to provide cover for the troops from the fire of the main fortress.

Lunette A work placed on both sides of a ravelin to defend it, e.g. Picurina and the San Roque.

Palisades Strong stakes of wood about nine feet long driven into the ground usually in the covered way, about a yard from the parapet of the glacis.

Parallel A place of arms. Deep trenches in which the troops who are working on the approaches to a fortified place can be supported. Normally about three parallels are dug.

Parapet A parapet is a bank of earth raised upon the outer edge of the rampart. Used to protect the besieged and to give cover to defenders to enable them to fire down into the ditch.

Rampart A great bank of earth around a town to secure and defend it.

Ravelin A work placed in front of a curtain wall and used to cover the flanks of a bastion.

Re-entrant The re-entrant angle is that which has its point inwards, sometimes called a tenail angle.

Salient Angle The outward pointing angle of a defensive work.

Saps Saps are trenches made and carried on under cover of gabions, fascines, etc. Pushed forward from the main parallel to establish batteries and other parallels.

Traverse Traverses are trenches with parapets slanting towards the enemy and are designed to hinder them from passing through any narrow place or passage.

Woolpacks Usually five feet high and about fifteen inches in diameter and filled with wool. Like gabions they were used to provide cover for the troops until proper lodgments were made.

Bibliography

Manuscript Sources

Duty Book of the French Garrison in Badajoz. (National Army Museum)
Baron Armand Phillipon's Commission. Taken after the fall of Badajoz.
(National Army Museum)
Memorandum for the attack on Badajoz. Mss. of Wellington's orders for
the assault. (Royal Engineers Museum, Chatham)

Published Sources

BANNATYNE, LT-COL. NEIL History of the Thirtieth Regiment, 1689–
   1881. (1923)
BELL MAJ-GEN. SIR GEORGE Rough Notes of an Old Soldier During
Fifty Years Service. (1869)
BELMAS J. Journaux de Sieges Faits ou Soutenas Par les Francais dans la
   Peninsule de 1807 a 1814.
BLACKWOOD'S MAGAZINE The Letters of Charles Von Hodenberg,
   K.G.L. March, 1913.
BLAKENEY, ROBERT A Boy In The Peninsular War. The Services, Adven-
   tures and Experiences of Robert Blakeney, Subaltern in the 28th Regi-
   ment. (1899)
BRETT-JAMES, ANTONY Life in Wellington's Army. (1972)
COOKE, CAPTAIN J. Memoirs of the Late War. Comprising the Personal
   Narrative of Captain Cooke, of the 43rd Light Infantry. (1831)
COOPER, JOHN SPENCER Rough Notes of Seven Campaigns in Portugal,
   Spain, France and America, during the years 1809–1815. (1896)
COSTELLO, EDWARD Adventures of a Soldier . . . Comprising Narratives
   of the Campaigns in the Peninsular under the Duke of Wellington, and
   the recent Civil Wars in Spain. (1841)
COWPER, COL. L. I. The Kings Own. The Story of a Royal Regiment,
   1680–1814.
DICKSON, SIR ALEXANDER The Dickson Manuscripts. Being Diaries,
   Letters, Maps, Account Books with various other papers of the late Maj-
   Gen. Sir Alexander Dickson, G.C.B., K.C.H., K.T.S., Royal Artillery.
   Series 'C'. From 1909–1818. (1908)
DONALDSON, JOSEPH Recollections of the Eventful Life of a Soldier.
   (1856)
DOUGLAS, MAJ-GEN. HOWARD An Essay on the Principles and Con-
   struction of Military Bridges and the Passage of Rivers. (1832)
FORTESCUE, HON. J. W. A History of the British Army.
GERWOOD, LT-COL. The Dispatches of Field Marshal The Duke of
   Wellington, K.G. During His Various Campaigns in India, Denmark,
   Portugal, Spain, The Low Countries and France, From 1799–1818.
   (1837–38)

GRATTAN, WILLIAM Adventures of the Connaught Rangers From 1808 to 1814. (1847)

GREEN, WILLIAM Brief Outline of the Travels and Adventures of William Green during a period of 10 years in Denmark, Germany and the Peninsular War. (1858)

GUEDALLA, PHILIP The Duke. (1940)

HENRY, WALTER Surgeon Henry's Trifles; Events of a Military Life. (1843)

JENNINGS, WILLIAM A General System of Defence, With One General Rule for Erecting Fortifications. (1804)

JONES, COL. J. T. Journal of the Sieges Undertaken by the Allies in Spain in the years 1811 and 1812. (1814)

KINCAID, CAPT. J. Adventures in the Rifle Brigade in the Peninsular, France and the Netherlands, from 1809–1815. (1830)

KNOWLES, ROBERT The War in the Peninsular. Some Letters of Lt. Robert Knowles, a Bolton Officer. (1909)

LAMARE, COL. An Account of the Second Defence of The Fortress of Badajoz By The French in 1812. (1824)

LAWRENCE, WILLIAM The Autobiography of Sergeant William Lawrence, a Hero of the Peninsular and Waterloo Campaigns. (1886)

LONGFORD, ELIZABETH Wellington, The Years of the Sword. (1973)

MacCARTHY, JAMES Recollection of the Storming of the Castle of Badajoz. A Personal Narrative. (1836)

MAXWELL, W. H. Peninsular Sketches; By Actors on the Scene. (1845)

McGRIGOR, SIR JAMES The Autobiography of Sir James McGrigor, Bt. Late Director General of the Army Medical Department. (1861)

MULLIE, M. C. Biographie des Celebrites Militaires des Armées de terre et de mer, de 1789 a 1850.

NAPIER, W. F. P. History of the War in the Peninsular and in the South of France, From the Year 1807 to the Year 1814. (1828)

OMAN, CHARLES A History of the Peninsular War. (1902)

OMAN, CHARLES Wellington's Army. (1912)

ROBINSON, H. B. Memoirs of Lt-Gen. Sir Thomas Picton, G.C.B. (1836)

ROGERS, COL. H. C. B. Wellington's Army. (1979)

SIMMONS, GEORGE A British Rifleman. The Journals and Correspondence of Maj. George Simmons, Rifle Brigade, during the Peninsular War and the campaign of Waterloo. (1899)

SMITH, HARRY The Autobiography of Sir Harry Smith, Bt. of Aliwal on the Suthej, G.C.B.

SURTEES, WILLIAM Twenty-Five Years in the Rifle Brigade. (1833)

WELLER, JAC Wellington in the Peninsular. (1962)

WINDROW, M. AND EMBLETON, G. Military Dress of the Peninsular War, 1808–1814. (1974)

WROTTESLEY, LT-COL THE HON. G. Life and Correspondence of Sir John Burgoyne, Bt. (1873)

Index

Agueda, (River); 43.
Albuera, 6, 19, 25, 47, 49.
Alcacer do Sol, 8.
Aldea Gallega, 11.
Almeida, 42.
Alten, Victor Von, 7.
Argaum, 1.
Assaye, 1.
Austerlitz, 18.

Badajoz, 5-7, 9, 11, 14-15, 18-19, 24-25,
    30, 35, 37-38, 41, 43, 47-49, 53-54,
    64, 96-97, 100-101, 103, 105-108,
    112-113, 115-118.
Barbot, 47.
Baylen, 1.
Bell, George, 62.
Beresford, Lt.Gen, 6, 18, 25.
Berkley, Admiral, 8.
Billion, Chief de Battalion, 42.
Blakeney, Robert, 60, 98, 105, 113.
Bowes, Maj-Gen, 29, 115.
British Army, (Divisions), First, 7.
    Third, 14, 18, 25, 37, 50, 54, 67, 92,
    103, 110, 115.
    Fourth, 18, 25, 50, 58-59, 60, 90, 115.
    Fifth, 7, 15, 35-36, 43, 49, 112, 115.
    Light, 18, 25, 37, 50, 58, 60, 90-92,
    115.
    (Cavalry), 1st Hussars (King's German
    Legion), 7.
    Royal Corps of Sappers and Miners,
    117.
    Royal Military Artificers, 14.
    (Regiments), 4th King's Own Foot, 83,
    85, 104, 108,
    5th Foot, 74, 78, 80, 103.
    7th Royal Fusiliers, 54, 58.
    30th Foot, 83.
    38th Foot, 83, 85.
    43rd Light Infantry, 60, 64, 66, 101.
    44th Foot, 83.
    45th Foot, 69, 74, 99, 115.
    48th Foot, 50, 54.
    52nd Light Infantry, 64, 115.
    60th Rifles, 67.
    74th Foot, 37.
    77th Foot, 78.
    83rd Foot, 78, 109.
    88th Connaught Rangers, 36, 79, 103,
    106, 108.
    94th Foot, 68, 73, 78.
    95th Rifles, 63-64, 92, 102, 115.
    King's German Legion, 101.
Brooke, Lt.Col, 83, 85.

Brooks, Rifleman, 34.
Brown, William, 32, 69, 99.
Burgoyne, Major, 32, 68.
Burgoyne, General, 9.
Burrard, General, 1.
Busaco, 4.

Cadiz, 14-15, 18.
Cameron, Col, 111.
Campbell, Col, 67, 78, 80.
Campo Mayor, 105.
Canch, Grenadier, 74.
Castello Branco, 7.
Caya, (River), 15.
Cerro de San Miguel, 25.
Ciudad Rodrigo, 6-7, 14, 27, 48, 52.
Colville, Maj-Gen, 29, 50, 115.
Convention of Cintra, 1.
Cooke, Lt, 31, 40, 58, 62, 100, 115.
Cooper, John Spencer, 58.
Cordova, 43.
Corunna, 3.
Costello, Edward, 29, 34, 36, 59, 64,
    92-93, 96, 103, 106, 108-109, 112.
Crawley, Rifleman, 36.
Cuesta, General, 4.
Cuthbert, Capt, 32.

Dalrymple, General, 1.
Daricau, Gen, 43.
De Grasse, Capt, 88-89.
De Ruffey, Lt, 24, 50.
Dickson, Alexander, 7-8, 14.
Donaldson, Joseph, 68, 73, 105, 107, 112.
Douro, Battle of, 3.
Drouet, Gen, 15, 43.
Duhamel, Lt, 42.

Elvas, 7, 11, 14-15, 25, 47.
Estremadura, 15, 18.

Fleming, Sgt, 111.
Fletcher, Col, 14, 25, 32, 49.
Forbes, Doctor, 81.
Freineda, 7.
French Army, (Cavalry),
    21st Chasseurs a Cheval, 24.
    26th Dragoons, 31,
    (Infantry Regiments), 9th Light
    Infantry, 24, 42, 80.
    28th Light Infantry, 24, 85.
    58th Regiment, 24, 45, 50, 85.
    64th Regiment, 24.
    88th Regiment, 24, 47, 80.
    103rd Regiment, 24, 40, 47.

Hesse D'Armstadt Regiment, 24, 40, 47, 81.
Fuentes D'Onoro, 6.

Gardiner, 14.
George II, 9.
Gipps, Lt, 38, 40.
Glubb, 14.
Graham, Lt.Gen, 43.
Grattan, William, 31, 38, 43, 47, 59, 64, 74, 93, 97, 104.
Green, William, 52, 56, 62-63.
Grenada, 15.
Guadajore, 43.
Guadiana, (River), 18, 20, 25, 35-36, 43, 51, 54, 105, 111, 113, 118.

Harvey, Brig-Gen, 115.
Henry, Walter, 105, 110.
Hill, Lt-Gen, 43, 49.
Holcombe, 14.
Holloway, Capt, 38, 40.
Hopkins, Edward, 88, 104.
Hythe, 1.

Joseph, King of Spain, 6.
Joudain, Gen, 4.
Junot, Gen, 1.

Kellerman, Gen, 116.
Kempt, Maj-Gen, 29, 37, 67, 74, 115.
Kincaid, John, 25, 27, 29, 35, 51, 93, 107-108, 111.
Kingsmill, Parr, 79.
Knoller, Col, 24.
Knowles, Robert, 54, 56.
Kulm, Battle of, 117.

La Llerena, 43, 47.
Lamare, Col, 18, 41-42, 44, 46-47, 56, 89.
Lavigne, Lt, 31, 80.
Lawrence, William, 30-31, 100.
Lefaivre, Capt, 21.
Leith, Lt-Gen, 35-36, 49, 85, 89, 118.
Leon, 1.
Lery, Gen, 116.
Lindsay, Capt, 40.
Lisbon, 5, 8-9.
Liverpool, Lord, 14, 116.
Lurat, 47.

MacCarthy, James, 28, 33, 36, 53, 67-68, 72-73.
MacPherson, Lt, 74, 78, 80-81.
McGrigor, Sir James, 27, 81, 101, 106.
McLeod, Col, 64, 81, 115.
Madrid, 1-2, 6.
Maistre, 47.
Maillet, Lt, 50.
Malaga, 43.
Malheste, Capt, 85.
Maransin, 43.
March, Lord, 81.
Marcillac, Capt, 41.
Marmont, Marshal, 6-7, 15, 18, 43, 116.

Massena, Marshal, 4-6.
Merida, 49.
Meynhart, Capt, 24.
Michel, Lt, 24.
Montes, Gen, 43.
Moore, Sir John, 1-3.
Morena, 43.
Mulcaster, Capt, 36.

Napier, William, 38, 115.
Napoleon, 1-2, 4-5, 15.
Nicholas, Capt, 66.
Niza, 7.
Nugent, Col, 85.

Oates, 39.
O'Hare, Maj, 111, 112.
Olivenza, 25.
Oman, Charles, 97.
Oporto, 8.
Orange, Prince of, 81.

Packenham, Sir Edward, 74, 78.
Pardaleras, Fort, 19-20, 24, 50.
Percival, Capt, 110.
Phillipon, Baron Armand, 18, 24-25, 31-32, 35, 40, 42-43, 47, 49-50, 80, 88, 97, 106, 116-118.
Picton, Lt-Gen, 29-30, 32, 50, 67-68, 74, 89, 115, 118.
Picurina, Fort, 19, 24-25, 27, 31, 37-42.
Pineau, Col, 24.
Piper, Major, 85, 88.
Portalegre, 7.
Portuguese Army, Power's Division, 43, 51.
    3rd Elvas Regiment, 14.
    15th Regiment, 85.
Power, Brg, 51, 110.
Powis, Capt, 37, 40.

Raulef, Lt, 24.
Rettberg, 14.
Ridge, Col, 74, 79.
Rivellas, (River), 22-23, 42, 50, 54, 68, 118.
Ronda Hills, 43.

Sabagul, 6, 7.
Saintourners, Capt, 45.
Saint-Victor, Capt, 81.
Salamanca, Battle of, 2.
San Antonio, (Bastion), 49, 72.
San Christobal, (Fort), 18-19, 24, 35, 40-41, 47, 51, 88, 106, 108, 118.
San Pedro, (Bastion), 49, 72.
San Roque, (Fort), 19, 22, 31, 34-35, 40, 42, 44-45, 51, 54, 56, 67, 93, 118.
San Sebastian, 117.
San Vincente, (Bastion), 50, 83, 85, 88, 104, 110, 115, 118.
Santa Maria, (Bastion), 41, 44-45, 47, 49-50, 66, 113, 118.
Schmalkalder, Chief de Battalion, 81.
Schulz, Adj-Gen, 81.
Setubal, 6-7.

Seville, 5, 34, 43.
Shaw, Maj, 37, 39-40, 66.
Shorncliffe, 1.
Sierra del Viento, 25, 49.
Simmons, George, 45, 63, 90-91, 102, 111.
Smith, Harry, 28, 60, 108.
Smith, Lady, 108-109.
Somerset, Lord Fitzroy, 106.
Soult, Marshal, 3, 5-6, 14-15, 19, 43, 47, 49, 116.
Squire, Major, 32.
Stanway, Lt, 38, 40.
Surtees, William, 107, 110-111.

Taggart, Lt, 60.
Tagus, (River), 1, 4.
Talavera, 4, 18, 27, 31, 42, 102.
Talavera de Real, 49.
Tete du Pont, (Fort), 18-19, 42, 118.
Thierry, Col, 24, 37, 40.
Thompson, Capt, 27.
Thomson, Major, 36.
Torrens, Lt-Col, 117.
Torres Vedras, (lines of), 4.
Tracey, Rifleman, 34.

Trinidad, la, (Bastion), 19, 31, 35, 41-42, 44-47, 49-50, 60, 64, 110, 113, 118.
Truilhier, Chief de Battalion, 24, 42.
Tyler, Lt, 82.

Vallon, Lt, 24.
Vandamme, Gen, 117.
Vauban, Sebastian de la Prestre, 11.
Veiland, Gen, 24-25, 31, 40, 47, 80, 85, 88.
Verle, Lunette, 18-19.
Victor, Gen, 4.
Villa Vehla, 7.
Villain, Capt, 24.
Vimiero, Battle of, 1.
Von Hodenberg, Charles, 101, 113.

Walker, Gen, 83, 85, 89.
Waterloo, Battle of, 117.
Wellington, Duke of, 1, 3-7, 11-12, 14-15, 18, 22, 25, 32, 35-36, 41-47, 49-50, 64, 66, 72, 81-82, 89, 91, 106, 108, 110, 115-117, 119.
Williams, Col, 67-68.
Wilson, Maj, 50, 54.